PIECING TOGETHER THE PROSPERITY PUZZLE

BY GREGG WEAR

Unless otherwise indicated, all Scripture quotations are taken from the *King James Version* of the Bible.

PIECING TOGETHER THE PROSPERITY PUZZLE

TABLE OF CONTENTS

SECTION 1 -- FINANCIAL PROSPERITY IS THE
WILL OF GOD

SECTION 2 -- NEEDS VS. ABUNDANCE
(Does God meet only our needs?)

SECTION 3 -- STUMBLING BLOCKS
TO PROSPERITY

- Table of Contents continued next page

TABLE OF CONTENTS, CONTINUED

SECTION 4 -- GUIDELINES TO FINANCIAL PROSPERITY *GOD'S* WAY

Other Books by Gregg Wear

Untangling The Healing Crisis

This 206 page book answers the many questions people ask about divine healing. Divine healing is unmistakably the will of God for all, but what about Job? Paul's thorn in the flesh? Timothy's weak stomach? The man born blind in John 9? This is written in such a way to help the reader understand why God wants them to be healed and *how* healing can be received.

Faith -- The Supernatural Connection

This 200 page book explains how to make the supernatural connection with God in prayer. Prayer and faith is not difficult, it simply has to be learned. The reason it has seemed difficult for some is because of a lack of understanding from the Bible on *how* to believe and *how* to get strong faith. This book makes faith easy to grasp.

Beating The Blame Game

This 200 page book proves from the Bible that God is not responsible for the sorrow and tragedy in the world. Much confusion exists in the Body of Christ on the subject of suffering, tests, and trials. The good news is, God is not responsible for disease, poverty, and tragedy. This book will help the reader to grasp the goodness of God and how to rise above the circumstances of life.

The price of each book is $10.00, plus $2.00 for shipping and handling. To order, write:

Gregg Wear Ministries
P.O. Box 1193
Sedalia, MO 65302

PIECING TOGETHER THE PROSPERITY PUZZLE

SECTION 1

FINANCIAL PROSPERITY IS THE WILL OF GOD

Introduction to Section 1

...thou shalt remember the Lord thy God; for it is he that giveth thee power to get wealth...
- Deuteronomy 8:18

The blessing of the Lord, it maketh rich, and he addeth no sorrow with it.
- Proverbs 10:22

Financial prosperity is the will of God for every one of God's children. Psalms 35:27 plainly states, "*...Let the Lord be magnified, which hath pleasure in the prosperity of his servant.*" III John, v.2 also states, "*Beloved, I wish above all things that thou mayest prosper...even as thy soul prospereth.*" Without a doubt, every child of God has a right to prosper materially and financially.

Unfortunately, some Christians have had a difficult time understanding this. Some of their churches either taught against financial prosperity, or rather they emphasized a gospel of "meager living." In other words, they taught it was okay to have a few material possessions, but not too many. If they possessed too much they might appear carnal or prideful.

1

As a result, if someone brought up the word "abundance" they were scared away. The word "prosperity" was changed from its truest meaning to a bland, watered-down version that eliminated any physical, material, and financial blessing and emphasized only the prosperity of the soul. But a quick cure for this kind of thinking is the verse I previously quoted, III John, v.2, -- *"Beloved, I wish above all things that thou mayest prosper...EVEN AS thy soul prospereth."*

Certainly God wants our souls to prosper, but equally important in God's eyes is our financial prosperity. The key phrase is, *"...even as thy soul prospereth."* If we'll take care of the inside, God will take care of the outside. God doesn't want our outside wealth to exceed our inside wealth, but neither does He want our outside wealth fail to meet our inside wealth.

EVEN AS OUR SOULS PROSPER

For example, if our outside wealth should exceed the growth and development of our souls, the temptation to yield to pride, and fall into the trap of self-exaltation and depend on one's own ability rather than God, is a definite, most probable danger. This is why Jesus said, *"...How hard is it for them that trust in riches to enter into the kingdom of God!"* (Mark 10:24). People who trust in riches have outside wealth without any inside wealth.

Where they have missed it is in their trust. It's not the riches that are wrong, it's the misguided trust that is wrong. Notice again what Jesus said, *"How hard is it for them that TRUST in riches to enter into the kingdom of God."*

2

FINANCIAL PROSPERITY IS THE WILL OF GOD

The person who _trusts_ in riches falls into the trap of thinking that money can buy them everything. They're so used to people being swayed by money, and they're so used to getting their own way every time they wave a few high dollar bills that they then think they can buy their way into heaven by giving a large donation to a charity or church, as if God is moved by large donations.

Quite frankly, such things sadden God. God doesn't look on the outside, God looks on the heart. That's why when the widow gave her two mites she scored more in heaven than did the largest offering given in the temple that particular day. Her motive in doing what she was doing came from a pure heart.

But this is not to say that God is against large offerings, and neither does it mean that God is against Christians being rich. After all, a rich disciple of Arimathea named Joseph gave an extremely expensive offering by donating a rich man's tomb that was hand carved in a rock (Matt. 27:60). What is most important to God is the priority and the motive of our heart. If our heart is right with God, and if we'll seek _first_ the kingdom of God and his righteousness, Jesus is all in favor of His people enjoying the creature comforts of life (Matt. 6:33).

DEFINITIONS OF PROSPERITY

Take note of the following definitions from "The New Lexicon Webster's Encyclopedic Dictionary of the English Language:"

prosper -- **to thrive, to achieve financial success**
prosperity -- **the condition of being prosperous, the condition of high economic activity**
prosperous -- **financially successful**

PIECING TOGETHER THE PROSPERITY PUZZLE

"The Random House Dictionary" definitions are as follows :

prosper -- to be successful, esp. financially
prosperity -- the state or condition of being successful, esp. financially
prosperous -- having or characterized by financial success

The Greek word translated "prosper" in III John, v.2, -- *"Beloved, I wish above all things that thou mayest PROSPER, even as thy soul prospereth,"* is *euodoo*, which is from two words, "good," and "journey," i.e. a good journey. "Strong's Exhaustive Concordance of the Bible" then adds, *"to succeed in business affairs."*

Simply put, in our journey through this life, God wants us to succeed in our business affairs, which in turn results in a condition of high economic activity and financial success, even as our souls succeed in spiritual affairs.

Clearly, as we grow and develop in our spiritual walk, our financial condition can correspondingly grow and develop. This is not to say that every rich person is a spiritual person, and this is not to say that every spiritual person is a rich person. **But this does mean that every spiritual person CAN be a rich person, because their inside condition is more important to them than their outside condition.**

4

FINANCIAL PROSPERITY IS THE WILL OF GOD

WORLD'S WAY VERSES GOD'S WAY

...Soul, thou hast much goods laid up for many years...   - rich farmer, Luke 12:19
...Thou fool, this night thy soul shall be required of thee...   - God, Luke 12:20

...Lord, thou deliveredst unto me five talents*: behold, I have gained beside them five talents more...
                                          - successful steward, Matt. 25:20
...Well done, thou good and faithful servant...
                                          - steward's lord, Matt. 25:21

*_The Open Bible, Expanded Edition,_ 1985, p. 327, tells us a talent of silver is 3,000 shekels. One shekel is valued at 4 days' wages of the common laborer. Thus, one talent of silver was worth 12,000 daily wages.

What does this mean in financial terms today? The wage of the common laborer today is approximately $100 a day, which is $500 a week, or $26,000 a year. $100 multiplied by 12,000 daily wages is $1,200,000. Five talents at $1,200,000 is $6,000,000. Thus, the faithful servant doubled his $6,000,000 to $12,000,000.

There are two kinds of riches shown here. One was condemned by God, one was commended by God. One did not have God's blessing, and one did have God's blessing. Obviously, there's nothing wrong with financial success, as Jesus commended the servant who did well financially. In fact, right here should be enough to show the person with an open mind that God is not opposed to financial increase. Actually, God _expects_ financial increase to take place among His people. The one servant who did nothing with his talent was denounced by his lord. At the very least he should have put it into the bank to gain interest (Matt. 25:27).

5

The difference between the rich farmer and the successful steward was not in the increase of wealth and riches, but it was in the condition of the heart, the motive for increase, and the number one priority in life. *The rich farmer missed it on all three counts.* His spiritual life was nil, his motive was for greed and selfishness, and his priority in life had nothing to do with the establishing of God's covenant in the earth.

THE HIGHEST PURPOSE FOR WEALTH AND RICHES

According to Deut. 8:18, the highest purpose for wealth and riches is for the spreading of the gospel. Notice:

...for it is he (God) that giveth thee power to get wealth, that he may establish his covenant which he swear unto thy fathers...
- Deuteronomy 8:18

If we'll make our number one priority in life the financing of the spreading of the gospel all around the earth, God will bring to pass in our lives this power to get wealth. I've come to the realization that I not only want to preach this gospel in these last days, I also want to be a part of financing this gospel in these last days. It's my heart's desire that every country, every tribe, and every tongue have the _repeated_ chance to hear a clear, simple presentation of the good news of the Lord Jesus Christ.

But since I'm not called to preach in other countries I can't go to other countries to preach. But, thank God, I've learned this, *I can be a part of financing other preachers who are called to go preach in other countries!* It takes incredibly huge sums of money to support the labourers in the harvest, not only here, but in other coun-

6

tries as well. The ultimate purpose for God bringing wealth into our hands is for the spreading of the gospel all around the world.

I've also learned this -- *the pipe that carries water to the thirsty can't help but get wet itself.* **If we'll be a pipe for God's finances to flow through for the spreading of the gospel we can't help but get wet ourselves with financial blessings!**

THE PURPOSE OF SECTION 1

This section is the first section in a 4-section book on Biblical, financial prosperity. My purpose in this section is to establish from the Word of God that financial prosperity is the will of God for all of God's children. I'll begin by looking at several real-life, Bible examples of prosperity, individuals who were very spiritual and who were also very rich. It's interesting that, in the minds of some people, being rich and being spiritual don't seem to go together. Generally, if you're "rich" you're considered to be a person of the world, maybe even a servant of Satan. If you're "spiritual" you're considered to be a poor person, at best a person of moderate means.

But the individuals in this section were not only wealthy people, they were also very spiritual, godly people. Some even played a critical role in the establish-ment of God's covenant in the earth in their day. Others, though their role was less pronounced, were used by God to be a blessing to the kingdom of God and the work of the ministry. Others yet, were able to use their God-given positions to influence the people of their day to leave their backslidden ways and return to God.

PIECING TOGETHER THE PROSPERITY PUZZLE

Open your mind and open your Bible, and as the Bereans did in Acts 17:11, study the scriptures earnestly to see if these things are true. If you've ever had any misconceptions or doubts about the Biblical message of prosperity, yet you've instinctively known in your heart that it is right and you've been wanting to believe, I trust that this book will be a part of erasing any doubts and straightening out any misconceptions you may have had.

Once you have it established in your heart and mind that God does indeed want you to prosper financially you'll be able to obey God's guidelines to move from where you presently are to where you want to be. And the more blessed you are, the more of a blessing you can be.

CHAPTER
1

JOSEPH OF ARIMATHEA

When the even was come, there came A RICH MAN of Arimathea, named Joseph, who also himself WAS JESUS' DISCIPLE:

- Matthew 27:57

I want the reader to notice that Joseph of Arimathea was *a rich man* AND *a disciple of Jesus*. This verse quickly dispels the notion that you have to be poor to be a believer. Just as surely as God wants our souls to prosper, God also wants us to prosper materially and financially as well.

God has two reasons for wanting to bless you financially -- #1) because He loves you, and #2) so that you can be a blessing to a lost and dying world. The good news of the gospel is, you don't have to be poor, you don't have to go without, and you don't have to suffer financially the rest of your life. It is the will of God that you be blessed financially in your pocket and purse, in your checkbook, and in your savings account (storehouse).

9

PIECING TOGETHER THE PROSPERITY PUZZLE

Some have said that God is not interested in any kind of prosperity except for the prosperity of the soul. This is one reason why I love III John, v. 2. Notice:

Beloved, I wish above all things that thou mayest prosper EVEN AS thy soul prospereth.

You see, God is concerned about another kind of prosperity *in addition* to the prosperity of the soul. To say that God is only interested in the prosperity of the soul is to deny the plain statement of the scriptures. The truth is, God takes great delight in His children prospering. It brings God pleasure when His children do well financially (Psalms 35:27).

It's interesting that some people get upset when the subject of prosperity comes up. And, I suppose, to a degree I can understand where they're coming from, simply because I came out of a religious mindset that equated poverty with being spiritual. In fact, certain groups have even taken a vow of poverty. In their thinking, if a person would have any money there's not any way that they could be a disciple of Jesus.

But Matthew 27:57 is just about as plain as it gets. Joseph of Arimathea was A RICH MAN <u>AND</u> A DISCIPLE OF JESUS. Clearly, you don't have to be poor to be a believer. One statement that God made to Joshua in Joshua 1:8 that I find to be very exciting is as follows:

This book of the law (God's Word) shall not depart out of thy mouth; but thou shalt meditate therein day and night, that thou mayest observe to do according to all that is written therein: *for then thou shalt make thy way <u>PROSPEROUS,</u> and then thou shalt have good <u>SUCCESS.</u>*

10

You see, according to God's Word, we should all want to prosper financially, we should all want to have good success, we should all want to be blessed when we're in the city and when we're in the field (Deut. 28:3), we should all want God's blessings overtaking us where we don't have room enough to contain them all (Mal. 3:10), we should all want to have God's blessings on our savings accounts (Deut. 28:8), and we should all want God's blessings on every business endeavor we set our hand to undertake (Deut. 28:8).

Others have said that people who believe in prosperity are only interested in cars, houses, and clothes.

But this is not true. Of course, I'm not denying that there are people out there who are immature in their Christian walk and who focus only on things like cars, houses, and clothes. But more often than not, many of these people who are now focusing on the "things" of life have gone without for so long and have been taught a "poverty gospel" their whole life, that when they hear the simple truth about Bible prosperity, it's so liberating and such a breath of fresh air to know that they don't have to be poor and that they don't have to feel guilty about living a prosperous lifestyle, that for a time they're focusing only on the "things."

Given enough time, they'll grow out of this temporary stage and come to the realization of a higher motive. *Without a doubt, our primary motive is in the establishing of God's covenant in the earth.* We're just saying that while we're establishing God's covenant in the earth, there's nothing wrong with having nice cars, nice houses, and nice clothes. (And this will be proved scripturally in chapter 7.)

PIECING TOGETHER THE PROSPERITY PUZZLE

Others, when the subject of prosperity comes up, immediately bring up the rich, young ruler. They say, *"Yes, but didn't Jesus tell the rich, young ruler to get rid of all that he had?"*

The answer is yes, *because his riches were keeping him from being a disciple of the Lord.* This is why it's so important to always read other verses in the Bible on the same subject. **You notice that Jesus didn't tell Joseph of Arimathea to get rid of all that he had in order to be a disciple.** Why? Because his riches were not keeping him from being a disciple of the Lord. As a result, he was RICH and A DISCIPLE.

That tells me then that if <u>your</u> priorities are correct, and if your motives are pure, there's nothing wrong with you being rich and being a believer. God is no respector of persons, <u>*and if Joseph of Arimathea was a rich person and a believer, that means you, too, can be a rich person and a believer.*</u>

This does away entirely with the notion that if you have any money it means you're less of a disciple. In fact, notice the word "also" in our text:

When the even was come there came a rich man of Arimathea, named Joseph, who <u>ALSO</u> himself was Jesus' disciple:
- Matthew 27:57

Obviously then, Joseph of Arimathea was among several others in this passage who were considered disciples of Jesus. Whenever I see the word "also" I always back up a few verses to see who or what this word is making reference to. So let's back up to verse 55:

12

JOSEPH OF ARIMATHEA

OTHERS IN THIS PASSAGE WHO WERE DISCIPLES

And many women were there beholding afar off, which followed Jesus from Galilee, ministering unto him: AMONG WHICH WAS MARY MAGDALENE...
- Matthew 27: 55,56

You'll remember that Mary Magdalene was the one who had seven demons cast out of her. Once she was set free she was a very spiritual woman. It's also believed that she was the one who anointed Jesus with the alabastor box of ointment and wiped his feet dry with her hair. Clearly, a very godly woman. Let's read on:

Among which was Mary Magdalene, AND MARY THE MOTHER OF JAMES AND JOSES...
- Matthew 27:56

This is talking about a woman who was a mother of two of the twelve disciples handpicked by Jesus to follow him. Like her two sons she, too, was a follower of Jesus. Again, another godly, spiritual woman. Let's read further:

Among which was Mary Magdalene, and Mary the mother of James and Joses, AND THE MOTHER OF ZEBEDEE'S CHILDREN.
- Matthew 27:56

This is talking about the mother of James and John, two more of the twelve disciples who were handpicked by Jesus to follow him. Again, another godly, spiritual woman who was a follower of Jesus.

In this one verse, Matthew 27:56, we find three women who were followers of Jesus, three women who were considered disciples of Jesus, and what follows next is verse 57:

When the even was come, there came a rich man of Arimathea, named Joseph, WHO ALSO HIMSELF WAS JESUS' DISCIPLE:

- Matthew 27:57

The point is, Mary Magdalene was considered a disciple of Jesus; Mary, the mother of James and Joses was considered a disciple of Jesus; the mother of Zebedee's children was considered a disciple of Jesus; AND A RICH MAN OF ARIMATHEA NAMED JOSEPH WAS ALSO CONSIDERED A DISCIPLE OF JESUS!

You notice that there's not any distinction made in this group that says any particular person was considered more or less of a disciple than the others. Joseph wasn't considered less of a disciple because he was a rich man. And he wasn't considered a better disciple because he was a rich man. But the inference is, Joseph was *just as much* a disciple as Mary Magdalene, he was *just as much* a disciple as Mary, the mother of James and Joses, and he was *just as much* a disciple as the mother of James and John.

He wasn't considered more spiritual because he was a rich man, and he wasn't considered more carnal because he was a rich man. *The plain fact is, he believed in Jesus, and the holy scriptures themselves call him a disciple of Jesus, MONEY AND ALL.* And if his money didn't make him any less spiritual, if his money didn't make him any less of a disciple, by YOU having money it won't make you any less spiritual and it won't make you any less of a believer!

14

JOSEPH OF ARIMATHEA

This notion of believers being considered carnal if they have any money is totally unfounded. Look at what a great blessing Joseph's riches enabled him to be to Jesus. He was able to provide Jesus with a rich man's tomb that was hand carved in a rock. And if you'll believe God for prosperity, you, too, can be a unique blessing to the kingdom of God in ways that blow the finite mind apart.

Prosperity doesn't make a person any less spiritual.
Prosperity doesn't make a person any more carnal.
Prosperity doesn't make a person any less of a believer.

Prosperity is just simply a tool. God wants to bless you financially because He loves you, and so you can be a blessing to the kingdom of God. Again, Joseph of Arimathea was a rich man <u>and</u> a disciple of Jesus. Matthew 27:57 is just about as plain as it gets -- you don't have to be poor to be a believer.

Let's take a look at some other prosperous Bible characters...

CHAPTER
2

HEZEKIAH
AND
UZZIAH

And in every work that he (Hezekiah) began in the service of the house of God, and in the law, and in the commandments, to seek his God, HE DID IT WITH ALL HIS HEART, AND PROSPERED.

- II Chronicles 31:21

You'll remember that Hezekiah was the one who turned his face to the wall and was healed. The prophet Isaiah showed up on his doorstep one day and told him to set his house in order because he was going to die. But because of answered prayer, not only was he healed, God added another 15 years to his life. And I think it would be safe to say, that out of all the kings that ruled over Israel and Judah, Hezekiah was in the top three of the most spiritual kings.

PIECING TOGETHER THE PROSPERITY PUZZLE

Let's take note of Hezekiah's prosperity:

And Hezekiah had <u>exceeding much riches</u>...
- II Chronicles 32:27

Whenever I see the word "exceeding" I always think of Ephesians 3:20 that says God is able to do <u>exceeding</u>, abundantly above all that we can ask or think. Now it would have been one thing to say that Hezekiah had *much* riches (and that would've been exciting), but it's an entirely different thing when it says, "*And Hezekiah had <u>exceeding</u> much riches.*" Evidently we're talking about a whole lot of riches. Let's notice further:

And Hezekiah had exceeding much riches and honor: and he made himself TREASURIES for SILVER, and for GOLD, and for PRECIOUS STONES, and for spices, and for shields, and FOR ALL MANNER OF PLEASANT JEWELS;
- II Chronicles 32:27

It's one thing to have silver, gold, precious stones, and all manner of pleasant jewels, but it's an entirely different matter when one has *so much* silver, *so much* gold, *so many* precious stones, and *so many* pleasant jewels *that he actually had to build treasuries just to contain them all.* Actually, the Hebrew word translated "treasuries" in this verse can also be translated "<u>store-houses.</u>" Notice the next verse:

Storehouses <u>also</u>...
- II Chronicles 32:28

In other words, Hezekiah not only built storehouses for silver, gold, precious stones, and pleasant jewels, but he also built storehouses for:

18

HEZEKIAH AND UZZIAH

"Storehouses also for the increase of corn, and wine, and oil: and stalls for all manner of beasts, and cotes for flocks.

"MOREOVER he provided him cities, and possessions of flocks and herds IN ABUNDANCE: for <u>GOD</u> had given him substance VERY MUCH."

- II Chronicles 32: 28,29

Notice the two phrases, "in abundance," and "very much." Again, I remind the reader of Ephesians 3:20 that says God is able to do exceeding, *abundantly* above all that we can ask or think. It's important to realize that God is a God of abundance.

Now there's something here that we need to think about -- Would God have given Hezekiah exceeding much riches if it would have made him *less* spiritual?

Of course not. God is not in the business of making people *less* spiritual. God's in the business of making people *more* spiritual.

Also, would God have blessed Hezekiah with silver, gold, precious stones, and pleasant jewels if it would have driven him *away* from God?

Of course not. God is not in the business of driving people *away* from Himself. God is in the business of *bringing* people closer to Himself. So evidently then, silver, gold, precious stones, and pleasant jewels DO NOT DRIVE PEOPLE AWAY FROM GOD, AND THEY DON'T MAKE PEOPLE LESS SPIRITUAL!

I realize, of course, this is contrary to a lot of religious thinking. But if money is the problem, or if riches is the problem, then God owed Joseph of Arimathea an apology,

19

and you know that Jesus would've told him to get rid of all his riches. Also, God wouldn't have blessed Hezekiah with exceeding much riches and honor. Notice that last phrase of v. 29 again:

> **...for <u>GOD</u> had given him substance very much.**
> **- II Chronicles 32:29**

This verse can't be explained away. It clearly wasn't *man* that made Hezekiah rich, and it clearly wasn't the *devil* that made Hezekiah rich to try to lure him away from God. This verse is also as plain as it gets. *It was none other than God himself who made Hezekiah rich.* Why? Because his heart, just like King David's, was right with God.

If we, too, will keep our heart right with God, and if we'll seek first the kingdom of God and his right-eousness, there's nothing wrong with all of these things being added unto us. All of these riches outlined in v.27, v.28, and v.29 were not fish hooks cast by the devil, *all of these riches were rewards that God bestowed upon Hezekiah because of his obedience* (II Chron. 31: 20, 21).

UZZIAH'S PROSPERITY

Sixteen years old was Uzziah when he began to reign, and he reigned fifty and two years in Jerusalem. His mother's name also was Jecoliah of Jerusalem.
AND HE DID THAT WHICH WAS RIGHT IN THE SIGHT OF THE LORD, according to all that his father Amaziah did.
AND HE SOUGHT GOD in the days of Zechariah, who had understanding in the visions of God: AND AS LONG AS HE SOUGHT THE LORD, GOD MADE HIM TO PROSPER. **- II Chronicles 26: 3-5**

HEZIKIAH AND UZZIAH

There are two key phrases in this passage that preface Uzziah's prosperity. #1) He did that which was right in the sight of the Lord (v.4), and #2) He sought God (v.5). There's no doubt that if we want to enjoy the same blessing that Uzziah enjoyed, then we, too, need to do that which is right in the sight of the Lord, and we need to seek God.

Clearly, the condition for Uzziah's prosperity is found in v.5 -- "...*as long as he sought the Lord, God made him to prosper.*" We can then safely say, if he had not sought the Lord, God would not have made him to prosper.

We see, then, that prosperity is conditional -- if your heart is right with God, God *wants* you to prosper. But if your heart is not right with God, then prosperity is not for you. You see, prosperity is a *reward*, it's a *blessing* for people who do serve the Lord.

This thinking that money is something corrupt and evil is totally unscriptural. Someone said, "*Yes, but I know of one scripture that says money is the root of all evil.*" No, the verse they *think* they're quoting is I Timothy 6:10, but it doesn't say that money is the root of all evil, it says the *LOVE of money* is the root of all evil. As one preacher has aptly put it, you can commit that sin and not have a dime!

HAVING LESS MONEY ISN'T THE ANSWER

For example, if having *less* money made people *more* spiritual, then all of the inner cities in our country and in the world would be safe, beautiful places, with great revivals taking place, with great spiritual influence. There wouldn't be any violence because there wouldn't be any gangs.

I'm sure the reader is well aware that the areas with the highest crime rates, the areas with the most violence, the areas with the highest murder rates, **and the areas with the least spiritual influence, are the inner cities.** Our inner cities have been going to hell in a hand- basket because of a <u>lack</u> of money. Obviously then, <u>less money doesn't make people more spiritual.</u>

But now let me add this. God has not given up on our inner cities. God couldn't get enough of the old believers to go into the city to preach, so God said, "*I'll just raise up a bunch of believers who were raised in the city. And I'll take the worst of the worst. And I'll put My Spirit on them, and I'll put My anointing on them.*"

Now there are ministers who were at one time prostitutes, pastors who were at one time drug addicts, evangelists who were at one time gang members, and they're raising their voices and they're now saying, "*You don't have to be poor anymore. You don't have to be sick anymore. And you don't have to live a hell on earth anymore. Jesus Christ paid the price, once and for all, and all you have to do is to believe it.*"

That is what's going to turn our inner cities around. It can't be done by a liberal in the White House, and it can't be done by a conservative in the White House. **The only thing that can turn our cities around is a revival in the land.**

One of the greatest revelations you'll ever receive is when you realize that God is 100% for you, He's 100% behind you, and if you know Jesus, He's 100% **in** you. God is not against you, and He's not against you having money. The key is verse 5, "<u>As long as he sought the Lord, God made him to prosper.</u>"

CHAPTER
3

THE PATRIARCHS

ABRAHAM

And Abram was very rich in cattle, in silver, and in gold.

- Genesis 13:2

Many people tend to think that the Old Testament saints were rich only in things like cattle, goats, sheep, and various livestock. And they certainly were rich in those things (as we'll see later in this chapter), but I want you to notice that Abram was not only rich in cattle, _he was also very rich in silver and gold._ Notice:

And Abram was very rich in cattle, in SILVER, and in GOLD.

- Geneses 13:2

Also, take note of the word "very,"

And Abram was VERY RICH...

- Genesis 13:2

"The Random House Dictionary" gives the definition for "very" as meaning, "in a high degree." So I just simply

23

inserted this definition in the place of the word "very," and Genesis 13:2 read like this:

And Abram was RICH IN A HIGH DEGREE. He was RICH in cattle IN A HIGH DEGREE, he was RICH in SILVER IN A HIGH DEGREE, and he was RICH in GOLD IN A HIGH DEGREE.

It's one thing to be rich, but it's quite another thing to be rich *in a high degree*. Think about what this is saying -- The father of our faith was VERY rich. The man who it says believed in God and it was counted to him for righteousness, was VERY rich. The one who was the first person to "believe" as the New Testament defines the term, was VERY rich.

Also, I want the reader to notice that God didn't tell Abram to get rid of all of his riches in order to believe. Thus, Abraham was wealthy *and* a believer. The same God who offered Abraham righteousness was the same God who made Abraham very rich. So it could be said, "Righteous" Abraham was also "very rich" Abraham. So, the good news of the gospel is, if your priorities are correct, you don't have to choose riches over salvation, nor do you have to choose salvation over riches. God is the source of *both* blessings, righteousness *and* prosperity.

Think about what this is saying -- The source of Abraham's riches was *none other than God Himself.* Abraham clearly said, "*I don't want it said that any man made me rich*" (Gen. 14:23). I like that.

The truth of the matter is, no man is going to make you rich anyway. Or if they do, there's going to be some kind of a string attached. They'll come to you for some favor that would violate your conscience, or they'll end up

24

hating you, or despising you, and causing you all kinds of problems. And Abraham was smart enough to realize this. So he didn't want it said that any man had anything to do with his riches. *It was God, and God alone, who was the source of Abraham's riches.* Listen to what Abraham's faithful servant said:

AND THE <u>LORD</u> HATH BLESSED MY MASTER GREATLY; and he is become GREAT: and <u>HE</u> (GOD) hath given him flocks, and herds, and SILVER, and GOLD, and menservants, and maidservants, and camels, and asses.

- Gen. 24:35

Again, the scripture is emphatic as to Who blessed Abraham with this great wealth. It was God. But though the above scripture mentions <u>*what*</u> God had given to Abraham, it doesn't say <u>*how much*</u> God had given to Abraham. For example, how large were these flocks? How large were these herds? How many camels did he own? How many donkeys did he have? How many menservants did he have? How many maidservants did he have? To understand the scope of just how great Abraham's household truly was, we have to go back to chapter 14. Notice:

And when Abraham heard that his brother was taken captive, he armed his TRAINED SERVANTS, born in his own house, THREE HUNDRED AND EIGHTEEN...
- Genesis 14:14

Here we see that Abraham had trained 318 of his servants for war. Evidently, because of the many skirmishes that would continually break out over land disputes, wells, greed, etc., Abraham realized the necessity to train some of his men with the ability to defend and to fight.

More to our point, this shows us that Abraham had 318 menservants!! Not just 318 servants, but 318 *men* - servants, not counting *maid*servants. But notice this also:

...trained servants, BORN IN HIS OWN HOUSE, three hundred and eighteen...
- Genesis 14:14

These 318 menservants were the children of other servants *already in Abraham's household!* This raises the number higher yet. How many husband/wife-servants did it take to bear 318 sons? It would be pure speculation -- 50 husbands/50 wives? 100 husbands/100 wives? How many daughters were produced? Were there also approximately 300 daughters born? How many males were born that weren't trained for war? *I think we could safely say that his household consisted of between 500 and 1,000 servants.* Easily.

Abraham's household was almost more like a community. The difference was, though, he was responsible for feeding, clothing, and housing all of his servants. He, obviously, didn't have them around solely to provide for them. *His purpose in having servants was to work for him by taking care of his flocks, herds, and farming his land!*

This gives us some insight into just how large his farming/ranching operation was. How many flocks and herds could this many servants take care of? The number would be incredibly high. As Genesis 24:35 states, God blessed Abraham *greatly*. Not even counting his gold and silver, Abraham was very rich in cattle alone (Gen. 13:2), plus flocks (of sheep?), camels, and donkeys.

Was Abraham a spiritual man? Most definitely yes. Was Abraham a rich man? Most definitely yes. Again, another scriptural witness that confirms the fact that not only is it possible to be rich and godly, God *wants* His people to be godly *and rich.* Continuing further, let's look at Abraham's son, Isaac...

ISAAC

Isaac was wealthy for two reasons, 1) he inherited his father's wealth, and 2) God prospered his farming.

1) By Inheritance.

Abraham had a number of children. From Sarah he had Isaac. From Hagar he had Ishmael. After Sarah died he married Keturah and had six sons -- Zimran, Jokshan, Medan, Midian, Ishbuk, and Shuah. It's obvious by his response to Ishmael's plight (Gen. 21:11) that he loved all of his children greatly. Of course, the fact that he was over 90 years old before his first son was born, and the fact that he had longed for children his whole adult life, it naturally predisposed a great affection for children when he finally would have them.

Nevertheless, he recognized that God's blessing rested on his lineage through Isaac. Thus, when he realized that his earthly pilgrimage was drawing to a close, he arranged for a way to bless all of his children. Notice:

But unto the sons of the concubines, which Abraham had, Abraham GAVE GIFTS, and sent them away from Isaac his son, while he yet lived, eastward, unto the east country.   - Genesis 25:6

He gave gifts to *all* of his children, and since the land was set apart for his seed through Isaac, he sent them to a land in the east. Not only did Abraham teach his children the precepts of God (Gen 18:19), he also took an active part in their prosperity. No doubt his gifts included silver, gold, various livestock, as well as an arrangement for some property from the inhabitants in the east.

Abraham was unique in that he taught his children financial *and* spiritual prosperity. Proverbs 13:22 states, "*A good man leaveth an inheritance to his children's children.*" Abraham left a twofold inheritance, spiritual and financial.

The greater portion of his wealth, though, was left for the seed of promise, Isaac. Notice:

And Abraham gave all that he had unto Isaac.
- Genesis 25:5

Abraham left his great riches of cattle, silver, and gold (Gen. 13:2) to Isaac. Quite obviously, Isaac was extremely wealthy, if for no other reason, because of his inheritance. But God had more in mind...

2) God prospered Isaac's farming.

A great famine was in the land after the days of Abraham. The inhabitants in the country were packing all of their belongings and leaving the country. They had no choice, as farming was the number one way to live.

Without rain the land was parched, the soil was dry, the creeks and streams were dry beds, and rivers were but a trickle. No crops could grow, vegetation had dried up, and herds and flocks could no longer graze. Isaac, too, realized that he must leave, and no doubt would have, yet God appeared to him and spoke:

And the Lord appeared unto him, and said, Go not down to Egypt...Sojourn IN THIS LAND, and I will be with thee, AND WILL BLESS THEE...
- Genesis 26: 2-3

No doubt Isaac was a good farmer, but the most skilled and knowledgeable farmer can't make anything grow without water in depleted, parched soil. Yet God made it clear that He was going to BLESS HIM IN THIS LAND.

What God had in mind was just as miraculous as the multiplying of the widow woman's pots of oil (II Kings 4:1-7), or the multiplying of the loaves and fishes. God was going to cause a miraculous harvest in conditions that screamed impossible. This was purposely designed to make a lasting impression in Isaac's mind that his prosperity was a *miraculous* prosperity. All he had to do was stay and sow. So, Isaac planted seed in the midst of this great famine.

Then Isaac sowed IN THAT LAND (the land of famine), and received in the same year A HUNDREDFOLD; and THE LORD BLESSED HIM.
- Genesis 26:12

How did the Lord bless him? *By causing a hundredfold increase under impossible circumstances.* As has been said over and over, what is impossible with man is possible with God (Mark 10:27). Isaac's great prosperity had nothing in the world to do with his natural ability, it had everything to do with God's supernatural ability. Then notice the very next verse:

29

And the man WAXED GREAT, and went forward, AND GREW until he became VERY GREAT: for he had possessions of flocks, and possession of herds, and great store of servants (Were these the servants who had been with Abraham? Most likely yes.)**: and the Philistines envied him.**

- Genesis 26:13-14

Several things to notice in verses 12 through 14:

a) Notice in verse 13 that Isaac "grew until he became very great." This means that his prosperity grew. It's nice to be "great," but it's even better to be "<u>very</u> great." His prosperity may not have happened overnight, but because he obeyed God's word it did come.

b) His prosperity grew because <u>God</u> blessed him. As wealthy as he was because of his inheritance, God wanted him to have a prosperity that was seperate and unique from his inheritance. God wanted Isaac to recognize that he was a blessed man, not just because of who his father was, *but most importantly, because the Lord was his God.*

c) Isaac became so extremely wealthy it says the Philistines envied him. Clearly, <u>God</u> was the source of his "great" prosperity. Again, another man who was godly and wealthy. Another witness that confirms the fact that not all wealthy people are ungodly, but with God's help, all godly people can be wealthy.

...godliness is PROFITABLE unto all things, HAVING PROMISE OF THE LIFE <u>THAT NOW IS</u>, and of that which is to come.

- I Timothy 4:8

Unbelievers can only have wealth in the life that now
30

is, whereas believers can have prosperity in the present life AND in the future life.

JACOB

Jacob's prosperity began with the transfer of the Abrahamic blessing to him. His father, Isaac, because of his advanced age, realized that he could possibly die any time. So, before he died he wanted to make sure that the "blessing of Abraham" (Gal. 3:14) would continue through his seed. In short, Isaac pronounced this blessing on Jacob:

28 Therefore GOD GIVE <u>THEE</u> of the dew of heaven, and the fatness of the earth, and plenty of corn and wine:
29 let people serve thee, and nations bow down to thee: be lord over thy brethren, and let thy mother's sons bow down to thee: cursed be every one that curseth thee, and blessed be he that blesseth thee.
- Genesis 27: 28,29

This blessing, the blessing of Abraham, can be found in more depth in Deuteronomy 28: 2-13. It's also interesting to note that this same blessing has been transferred to every person that has made Jesus Christ the Lord of their life (Gal. 3: 13-14, see chapter 5). Just as surely as the patriarchs enjoyed abundant prosperity, we, too, can enjoy abundant prosperity.

This blessing pronounced by Isaac was a 10fold blessing. Each blessing had to do with success and prosperity while on the earth. Although it's not recorded, this was the same blessing that Abraham passed down to Isaac, and in turn, was now passed down to Jacob. And though he didn't have a dime in the bank, so to speak, Jacob's prosperity was a settled issue from that day forward. It was now just a matter of time.

Jacob left his father's house and began working for Laban, his new, crooked, father-in-law. Not only did Laban swindle Jacob with his choice of a wife, but 10 times in seven years Laban changed Jacob's wages. Obviously, if Laban would've had the final word Jacob never would have gotten ahead. Jacob's circumstances, present and future, from the natural human standpoint, were not good.

But again, where man's ability is lacking, God's ability more than makes up the difference. This should be a lesson to all of us -- if we don't have the natural ability to prosper and succeed, *God is not limited to our natural abilities.* Jacob's prosperity was not going to have anything to do with his own natural ability.

God gave Jacob an idea *in a dream* on how to prosper:

And at the mating season, I had a dream, and saw that the he-goats mating with the flock were streaked, speckled, and mottled. Then, in my dream, the Angel of God called to me and told me that I should mate the white nanny goats with streaked, speckled, and mottled he-goats.
- Genesis 31: 10-12, The Living Bible

Jacob's prosperity came from a supernaturally inspired idea. Again, his prosperity had nothing to do with his own natural ability, his prosperity was because of something God did. All Jacob had to do was obey what God said to do. The end result of God blessing him is found in Genesis 30:43:

And the man (Jacob) increased EXCEEDINGLY, and had MUCH cattle, and maidservants, and menservants, and camels and asses.

- Genesis 30:43

God has many, many ways in which He can bless His people. The key seems to be in finding out what God is leading _us_ to do. Don't fall into the trap of trying to do what God has told someone else to do. As we're obedient in doing what _we_ are supposed to be doing, prosperity will surely come.

JOB

...Job...was perfect and upright, and one that feared God, and eschewed evil.
...this man was the GREATEST OF ALL THE MEN OF THE EAST.   - Job 1: 1,3

It's important to point out that Job was not poor because he was serving God, he was the richest man out of all the men in the east because he was serving God! Verse 10 of this chapter leaves no doubt that God was the One responsible for Job's prosperity:

...thou (God) hast blessed the work of his hands, and his substance is increased in the land.
- Job 1:10

As most every Christian knows, Job faced some severe trials. He lost his health, his family, and all of his possessions. He went from being the richest man to being one of the poorest men. But Job's faith eventually prevailed, and God blessed him with healing, with a new family, and gave him twice as much as he had before. Job's wealth is recorded in Job chapter 42:

PIECING TOGETHER THE PROSPERITY PUZZLE

So the Lord blessed the latter end of Job more than his beginning: for he had **FOURTEEN THOUSAND SHEEP**, and **SIX THOUSAND CAMELS**, and a **THOUSAND YOKE OF OXEN**, and a **THOUSAND SHE ASSES.**

- Job 42:12

I thought it might be interesting to put the modern day price equvalency on Job's livestock to get a rough idea of how much he was worth. (This is not counting any material possessions, money, or gold, only his flocks and herds.) Let's again list his animals:

14,000 sheep
6,000 camels
1,000 she asses
1,000 yoke of oxen

At the time of this writing, a yoke of broke oxen is worth between $3,000.00 to $4,000.00. Since he possessed 1,000 yoke of oxen, their price value would be between 3 and 4 million dollars. (Incidentally, these prices are the *average* prices. Based upon an animal's breeding, etc., the prices could be much, much higher.)

A she-ass, a.k.a. Jenny, is worth $1,000.00. Job possessed 1,000 she-asses for a value of 1 million dollars.

A broke male camel (in Biblical times a riding camel was a male camel) is worth between $5,000.00 to $6,000.00. If the 6,000 camels mentioned meant riding camels, their worth would be between 30 million dollars to 36 million dollars. If the 6,000 camels meant male and female, assuming 3,000 male and 3,000 female, their worth would be between 15 million dollars to 18 million dollars, not counting the worth of the female camels. If a

34

female camel is worth half the price of the male, 3,000 female camels would be worth between 7 1/2 million dollars to 9 million dollars. The combined camels would be worth between 22 1/2 million dollars to 27 million dollars.

A bred ewe is worth between $200.00 to $250.00. Again, I'm assuming his flock was half ewe and half lambs (a lamb is estimated at $70.00). If so, out of the 14,000 sheep, 7,000 were ewe and 7,000 were lambs. The ewe would be worth between $1,400,000.00 to $1,750,000.00, and the lambs would be worth $490,000.00, for a total value between $1,890,000.00 to $2,240,000.00.

1,000 yoke of oxen	=	3	to 4	million dollars
1,000 she asses	=	1		million dollars
6,000 camels	=	22 1/2	to 36	million dollars
14,000 sheep	=	app. 2		million dollars
Total Value		28 1/2	to 43	million dollars

Job, in modern day price equivalency on livestock alone, *was worth between 28 1/2 million dollars and 43 million dollars!* Notice verse 12 again:

SO THE LORD BLESSED the latter end of Job more than his beginning...
- Job 42:12

Without a doubt, the Lord God was the One responsible for Job's prosperity. It's sad, but many people, even Christians, think if a Christian has any wealth he must be a crook or a con. They equate Christianity with poverty. I've even heard people say with pride, "*The reason I'm poor is because I'm serving God.*" But notice the difference here, Job was not poor because he was serving God, **he was extremely wealthy because he was serving God**! At the continued risk of redundancy, it must be said again, another man who was godly **and rich.**

CHAPTER
4

DAVID
AND
SOLOMON

DAVID

...I have a PRIVATE TREASURE OF GOLD AND SILVER which I give for the house of my God:
- David, I Chronicles 29:3, The Amplified Bible

Most Christians are aware of David the shepherd boy, David the king, and David fighting Goliath, yet most Christians are unaware of David's extreme wealth. Surprising to most Christians is the fact that David was very, very wealthy. Out of his own *personal* treasury David donated to the future construction of the temple an amount over $62,000,000,000.00 (62 billion dollars)!! Let's take a look at this contribution:

3   Moreover, because I have set my affection to the house of my God, I have of <u>MINE OWN PROPER GOOD</u>, of gold and silver, which I HAVE GIVEN TO THE HOUSE OF MY GOD, over and above all that I have prepared for the holy house.

4   Even THREE THOUSAND TALENTS OF GOLD, of the gold of Ophir, and SEVEN THOUSAND TALENTS OF REFINED SILVER, to overlay the walls of the houses withal:

- I Chronicles 29: 3-4

Out of his personal wealth David donated 3,000 talents of gold, and 7,000 talents of silver. Lest there be any doubt that this was David's *personal* fortune I've taken the liberty to quote from several other sources:

And now, because of my devotion to the Temple of God, I am giving ALL OF MY OWN PRIVATE TREASURES to aid in the construction...

- I Chron. 29:3, *The Living Bible*

Besides, in my devotion to the temple of my God I now give MY PERSONAL TREASURES of gold and silver...

- I Chron. 29:3, *New International Version*

...I have a PRIVATE TREASURE of gold and silver which I give for the house of my God:

- I Chron. 29:3, *The Amplified Bible*

...I possess a PRIVATE TREASURE of gold and silver...

- I Chron. 29:3, *James Moffatt Translation*

...because I delight in the house of my God, I give MY OWN PRIVATE STORE of gold and silver...

- I Chron. 29:3, *The New English Bible*

DAVID AND SOLOMON

Clearly, *this contribution was from David's **personal** account.* With this in mind let's examine what this contribution meant in financial terms. Some of the financial figures you're getting ready to read, **to the uninformed mind,** will seem almost outlandish, so it will be necessary to detail at how such figures were arrived.

I'll never forget the day when I realized the full scope of what the scriptures reveal concerning David's wealth. Why this hadn't been preached before can only be explained by the small, limited thinking that has plagued the Church. God is such a big God, that to not think big and to not believe big is detrimental to our every Christian endeavor. Because of the greatness of the work in front of us, it's time for God's people to greatly believe. With correct teaching we *can* fulfill the great commission to reach the world.

DAVID'S WEALTH IN MODERN DAY FIGURES

The wealth that David *personally* possessed is indeed astronomical. Let's look at this offering in modern-day figures:

To begin, *The Open Bible, Expanded Edition*, pg. 327, tells us a talent of silver is 3,000 shekels. (All Bible study aids agree with this fact.)

A shekel, according to *The Open Bible, Expanded Edition*, tells us a shekel is equivalent to 4 days' wages.*

* Most Bible study aids agree with this fact also, however, I found one Bible Dictionary that stated a shekel was worth 2 days' wages. To find out whether a shekel was worth 4 days' wages or 2 days' wages we have to cross reference two scriptures. 1) In Exodus 30:11-16,

every male 20 years of age and older was required to give *half a shekel* for the service of the tabernacle. 2) In Matthew 17:24-27, verse 25 states, "Doth not your master pay *tribute*?" In *Bible Manners and Customs*, 1972, pg.354 by James M. Freeman, it says, "*This was not the tax for the support of the civil government, but the half-shekel tax for the support of the temple-service, which every Jew was expected to pay.*"

The Greek word in verse 25 translated,"*tribute,*" is "*didrachma,*" "Doth not your master pay the *didrachma?,*" which is the half-shekel temple tax. Then, *Eerdman's Handbook to the Bible,* pg. 109, tells us *1 didrachma* was worth *2 denarii* (*1 denarius* was one days' wage for the ordinary working man). Thus, *1 didrachma* was equivalent to *half a shekel*, or, 2 days' wages, *which confirms the fact that one shekel was worth 4 days' wages*.

Since 1 talent of silver is 3,000 shekels, and one shekel is 4 days' wages, **this would mean that one talent is 12,000 days' wages** (3,000 shekels X 4 day's wages).

At this point, we have to decide, in modern-day terms, what a day's wage is. If, for example, a day's wage is $50, which is $250 a week, or $13,000 a year, a person in today's world (U.S.) most likely would be living with some kind of government aid. I can't think of anyone who could live on such a pay without some kind of financial help. Thus, $50 could not be considered the common laborer's daily wage.

Based on today's figures, the common laborer's daily pay would have to be *at least* twice that amount, at $100 a day, or $26,000 a year. (I realize this figure is a subjective figure, and in some cities this pay would be considered very low, as the standard of living varies state to state and city to city.) Nevertheless, I think we could safely say this figure could be the ordinary salary of a young man. Admittedly, though, this is a conservative figure.

With this figure, _one talent of silver_ would equal $100 multiplied by 12,000 days' wages, which is **$1,200,000.** According to *The Open Bible, Expanded Edition,* pg. 327, the value of gold is 15 times the value of silver. Thus, _one talent of gold_ is valued at **$18,000,000.00** (18 million dollars). (At the time of this writing, the value of a troy ounce of gold is $350. This has held constant for the last 6 months or so. A troy ounce of silver is approximately $5.00. Thus, at the time of this writing, gold is 70 times the value of silver!!!! But in Bible days, gold was valued at 15 times the value of silver.)

Again, David donated 3,000 talents of gold and 7,000 talents of silver for the construction of the temple. To find the modern day dollar equivalency we simply multiply the corresponding dollar amount times the number of talents:

3,000 talents of gold
at $18,000,000.00 each...................$54,000,000,000.00

7,000 talents of silver
at $1,200,000.00 each......................$8,400,000,000.00

Total offering of gold & silver $62,400,000,000.00

Think about this, David donated $62,400,000,000.00 in gold and silver _out of his own private account._ Why? Because David set his affection on the things of God (v.3). **Because his motives and his priorities were pure, God was able to bring extreme wealth into his hands.** This should be a great lesson to all of us. *What is even more startling is the fact that his son, Solomon, greatly surpas-*

sed even himself.

DAVID'S GIVING MOTIVATED OTHERS TO GIVE

After David had given this great financial gift, others in the kingdom were motivated to give as well:

6 Then the <u>chief</u> of the fathers and <u>princes</u> of the tribes of Israel, and the <u>captains</u> of thousands and of hundreds, with the <u>rulers</u> of the king's work, OFFERED WILLINGLY.

7 And gave for the service of the house of God of gold FIVE THOUSAND TALENTS and TEN THOUSAND DRAMS (a gold Persian daric worth $1,280.00 each, *The Open Bible, Expanded Edition, pg. 327*)**, and of SILVER TEN THOUSAND TALENTS, and of BRASS EIGHTEEN THOUSAND TALENTS, and ONE HUNDRED THOUSAND TALENTS OF IRON.**

- I Chronicles 29: 6-7

This is what the offering from David's key leaders (his chief, his princes, the captains, and the rulers) added up to:

```
5,000 talents of gold
  at $18,000,000 each.................$90,000,000,000.00
10,000 talents of silver
  at $1,200,000 each..................$12,000,000,000.00
10,000 drams
  at $1,280 each...........................$12,800,000.00
18,000 talents of brass (approximate)...$2,000,000.00
100,000 talents of iron (approximate)....$2,000,000.00
```

Total Value $102,016,800,000.00

Again, think about this, David's key leaders willingly gave over **102 BILLION dollars** to the work of God!!! One commentary made the statement that they must have had a lot of wealthy people in the kingdom. I don't think there's much doubt about this. But it's important to realize that the reason God brought this wealth into their hands was because *these people were givers.* Notice:

Then the people rejoiced, for that they offered willingly, BECAUSE WITH PERFECT HEART THEY OFFERED WILLINGLY TO THE LORD:
- I Chronicles 29:9

RICHES COME FROM GOD, SO SAYS DAVID

David then said:

BOTH RICHES AND HONOUR COME OF THEE, and thou reignest over all; and in thine hand is power and might; and IN THINE HAND IT IS TO MAKE GREAT, AND TO GIVE STRENGTH *UNTO ALL.*
- I Chronicles 29:12

David was acknowledging the fact that the reason they were rich was because it came from the hand of God. Again, *they were not poor because they were serving God, they were rich because they were serving God.* **In that one day over 164 BILLION dollars was given for the work of God from PERSONAL fortunes.**

I think the reader will find this to be interesting as well. You'll remember, in I Chronicles 29:3 David made mention that his offering of $62,400,000,000.00 was *over and above* what he had already prepared. Look again:

Moreover, **because I have set my affection to the house of my God, I have of mine own proper good, of gold and silver, which I have given to the house of my God, <u>OVER AND ABOVE</u> ALL THAT I HAVE PREPARED FOR THE HOLY HOUSE.**

- I Chronicles 29:3

MONEY DAVID HAD PREVIOUSLY PREPARED

Take note of what David had previously prepared for the temple back in chapter 22:

Now, behold, in my trouble I have prepared for the house of the Lord an HUNDRED THOUSAND TALENTS OF GOLD, and a THOUSAND THOUSAND (ONE MILLION) TALENTS OF SILVER; and of BRASS and IRON WITHOUT WEIGHT; FOR IT IS IN ABUNDANCE...

- I Chronicles 22:14

```
100,000 talents of gold
  at $18,000,000.00 each..........$1,800,000,000,000.00
1,000,000 talents of silver
  at $1,200,000.00 each...........$1,200,000,000,000.00
                                  ─────────────────────
          Total     $3,000,000,000,000.00
```

David had previously prepared <u>3 **TRILLION** DOLLARS</u> in gold and silver for the work of the temple!!!!! As for the brass and iron, it states that there was so much it hadn't even been weighed to know its worth. In fact, *evidently there was still much, much more gold and silver that hadn't even yet been weighed and counted.* Notice:

Of the GOLD, the SILVER, and the brass, and the iron, THERE IS NO NUMBER...

- I Chronicles 22:16

Without a doubt, David was prosperous, his country (kingdom) was prosperous, and his people were prosperous. David gave the key to his success to his son, Solomon, in verse 13. Clearly, he was well aware of Deuteronomy 28 and Joshua 1:8.

Then shalt thou PROSPER, *if thou takest heed to fulfill the statutes and judgements which the Lord charged Moses with concerning Israel:* **be strong, and of good courage; dread not, nor be dismayed.**
- I Chronicles 22:13

According to David, if we should live according to God's statutes and judgements, prosperity will result, providing we're being strong and of good courage. *David plainly stated that riches, honour, greatness, and strength is God's will **FOR ALL*** (I Chron. 29:12).

SOLOMON

...and I (God) will give thee riches, and wealth, and honour, *such as none of the kings have had that have been before thee, neither shall there any after thee have the like.*
- II Chronicles 1:12

Solomon was the richest man that ever lived. And he was rich because **God** made him rich, *"...and I (God) will give thee riches..."*. I Kings 10:23 states, *"So King Solomon exceeded all the kings of the earth for riches..."*.

A *partial* list of his wealth in gold is as follows:

And king Hiram sent to the king SIXSCORE (120) TALENTS OF GOLD.
- I Kings 9:14

45

And they came to Ophir, and fetched from thence GOLD, FOUR HUNDRED AND TWENTY TALENTS, and brought it to King Solomon.
- I Kings 9:28

And she (Queen of Sheba) gave the king AN HUNDRED AND TWENTY TALENTS OF GOLD...
- I Kings 10:10

Now the WEIGHT OF GOLD that came to Solomon in one year was SIX HUNDRED THREESCORE AND SIX TALENTS OF GOLD,
- I Kings 10:14

```
120 talents of gold
at $18,000,000.00 each...........$2,160,000,000.00
120 talents of gold
at $18,000,000.00 each...........$2,160.000,000.00
420 talents of gold
at $18,000,000.00 each...........$7,560,000,000.00
666 talents of gold
at $18,000,000.00 each.........$11,988,000,000.00
```

Total Value $23,868,000,000.00

I emphasize that this is a *partial* list. In I Kings 10:16-29, this passage mentions 200 targets of beaten gold: 600 shekels of gold for each target (v.16), 300 shields of beaten gold: 3 pounds of gold for each shield (v.17), a throne of ivory overlaid with gold (v.18), 14 statues of lions around the throne (gold?)(v.19-20), all drinking vessels were gold (v.21), and *every three years* his navy brought *additional gold, silver, and ivory* (v.22).

Also, this does not include the wealth of his *precious stones* (I Kings 10:10), nor the *yearly* deluge of presents

46

from all around the world of gold, silver, and various livestock (I Kings 10:25). Also not included are the chariots and horses (I Kings 10: 26,29).

In fact, the riches were so abundant in Jerusalem it states:

And the king made SILVER and GOLD at Jerusalem AS PLENTEOUS AS STONES.
- II Chronicles 1:15

What Solomon's total wealth actually added up to is difficult to figure. Suffice it to say, the scripture plainly states that no king before or after was as wealthy as he.

SUMMARY

Up to this point, we've looked at a number of real-life Bible examples of prosperity. Over and over we've seen the phrase, "*God made them rich.*" Terms were used, such as, "very rich," "very great," "increased exceedingly," "rich disciple," "prosper," etc. Some were rich in farming/ranching, others were rich in gold and silver, and one, Joseph of Arimathea, was rich without any explanation. (Since he owned his tomb in the Jerusalem area, does this mean he lived in the city? Was he a city merchant?) Whatever, the scripture plainly states that he was a **rich** disciple.

We see here that God prospers His people in many different ways. *God is not limited to any one method.* God can prosper some through the stock market, some through business, some through farming, some through unusual and creative ideas, etc. Deuteronomy 28:8 brings out the fact that God will prosper whatever you set your hand to do. So it's important to DO something. *Unneces-*

sary risks are to be avoided, but with planning, ideas, time, and obeying God's laws of tithing and offerings, prosperity can be yours.

The definition for the word "rich," according to *The Random House Dictionary,* says, *"having wealth or great possessions, abundant or plentiful."* Did all of our examples have wealth and great possessions? Most definitely yes. Did all of our examples enjoy abundance and plenty? Most definitely yes.

Without a doubt, God wants His people to enjoy abundance and plenty. *God does not want any of His children to suffer lack or need.* The extent, though, to just *how much* abundance and *how much* plenty is obtained is decided by *how much* God's people are willing to believe God and use their faith. How far do they want to go with God concerning finances? Are they willing to *sow much* so they can *reap much*? (II Cor. 9:6, Proverbs 11:24, 22:9). Just how willing are they to be a *great* financial blessing to the kingdom fo God?

David is an excellent example concerning this. Look at what he was willing to do with his finances. No doubt this is why God brought great wealth into his hands. David could be trusted to bless the work of the ministry financially. His extreme willingness to give brought extreme wealth into his life.

I believe God will go just as far financially with His people as His people will believe and use their faith. Really, I don't think there should be any doubt about this. Deuteronomy 8:18 states, *"for it is he (God) that giveth thee power to get **wealth** THAT HE MAY ESTABLISH HIS COVENANT...".* It takes WEALTH to spread the gospel of the kingdom all around the world.

Quite frankly, the unsaved world is not going to use their wealth to do this.

The advancement of the kingdom of God comes from people who are already in the kingdom of God. But if the citizens in the kingdom of God _here on earth_ are dirt poor, then obviously the advancement of the kingdom of God is going to be impeded. And millions of people, even billions of people, who _could_ have been reached with the gospel, and who _would_ have been reached with the gospel, will continue to be lorded over by Satan and the kingdom of darkness.

So something has to change. _And one thing that has to change is the believer's pocketbook._ As much as you'd like to give $1,000,000 in a one-time offering for the spreading of the gospel, if you don't have an extra $1,000,000 to give, then you cannot give $1,000,000 in a one-time offering. But if God can make you _very rich_ in silver, in gold, in stocks, in business, in farming, etc., then God can use you in an even greater way to be a part of financing this great end-time revival.

It's difficult for some Christians to realize that God wants to _abundantly_ prosper His people. _But this kind of thinking has to change._ It's high time for God's people to prosper, **and to prosper abundantly.** The good news is, the curse of poverty is broken!

CHAPTER
5

REDEEMED FROM THE CURSE OF POVERTY

> For ye know the grace of our Lord Jesus Christ, that, though he was RICH, yet for your sakes he became POOR, that YE through his POVERTY might be RICH.
>
> **II Corinthians 8:9**

It's interesting how some denominational groups deny any verse in the Bible that would mention any physical or material blessing. In short, some groups of believers who don't believe in financial prosperity or divine healing say that any verse that promises a material, physical benefit should be interpreted to mean a _spiritual benefit only_. They usually look for a different meaning other than what's written, and say that God really meant something supposedly "deeper" than what the verse appears to say.

The problem with this kind of thinking, though, is that it eliminates the pure, simple presentation of God's Word saying what it means, and meaning what it says. In effect, it's taking the Bible out of the hands of the common man and telling him that when he reads his Bible he can't understand what he reads. Only a trained minister with "X" amount of years in seminary can understand the Bible. (This is what happened in the Middle Ages.) The end result is that it forces the everyday, working person into a position of relying solely on someone else for their spiritual growth.

And I strongly disagree with this! This is defeating the whole purpose of God in giving us His Word. The purpose of the Bible was, and is, to bring God's Word to the common, everyday person.

If you're facing a particular problem God wants YOU to be able to pick up a Bible and, with a little diligence, find the help you need. You don't have to have a special decoder to understand what the Bible is saying. God's Word simply means what it says, and says what it means. It was never meant to be difficult, it was meant to be taken at face value. Sin is sin, physical healing is physical healing, financial prosperity is financial prosperity, answered prayer is answered prayer, and what things soever you desire means what things soever you desire.

The reason I bring this up is because some of these people say that II Corinthians 8:9 only has *spiritual* connatations. That this verse means only that God sent Jesus so we could become rich spiritually. But what they've failed to do is to be consistent in their rendering of this verse in its entirety. Notice again:

For ye know the grace of our Lord Jesus Christ, that, though he was RICH, yet for your sakes he became POOR, that ye through his POVERTY might be RICH.
- II Corinthians 8:9

If, for instance, we were going to tag "spiritually" onto the end of this verse -- *"that ye might be rich spiritually,"*

52

we would have to be consistent in our insertion of this word and also insert it throughout the rest of this verse. If so, it would read like this:

For ye know the grace of our Lord Jesus Christ, that, though he was rich spiritually, yet for your sakes he became poor spiritually, that ye through his spiritual poverty might be spiritually rich.
                                    - incorrect rendering of II Cor. 8:9

Here's the problem -- This verse would then be saying that though Jesus was rich spiritually in heaven, <u>when He came to earth He became poor spiritually.</u> And, obviously, that theology wouldn't hold up in any seminary or Bible school.

When Jesus came to earth as heaven's ambassador he was most definitely NOT a spiritually poor person! He was all God and all man. He was the most spiritually alive individual on this planet. To perform the kind of miracles that the four gospels record Jesus performing, Jesus had to have been rich spiritually.

For example, a spiritually poor person could not have raised Lazarus from the dead. A spiritually poor person could not have cleansed a diseased, leper's skin. A spiritually poor person could not have healed blinded eyes from a man born blind. Obviously, <u>Jesus was the most spiritually rich person the earth had ever seen.</u>

I mean, if Jesus would have been poor spiritually, it would have been the disciples who would have said to Jesus, "*O ye of little faith.*" But I'm sure the reader can see the absurdity of such a statement. Jesus was the epitome of faith and spiritual development. <u>*It was the world that*</u>

was poor spiritually! Man's condition was one of spiritual death. This was the whole reason Jesus needed to come.

When Jesus came to the earth, he was showing a spiritually bankrupt world what a spiritually rich relationship with God could be. Jesus was spiritually rich in heaven before He came to the earth, He was spiritually rich while He was on the earth, He is spiritually rich in heaven at the present, and He will be spiritually rich for all of eternity. After all, He is God.

Thus, *it's absolutely impossible to interpret this verse as saying Jesus became poor spiritually.* It was a spiritually rich person who performed the incredulous miracles of calming the stormy wind and waves. It was a spiritually rich person who multiplied the loaves and the fishes to feed 5,000. It was a spiritually rich person who turned the water into wine. It was a spiritually rich person who raised the widow's son from the dead. It was a spiritually rich person who healed the sick by the multitudes. *Clearly, the only way to interpret this verse is in a material, financial context.*

THE CONTEXT IS ABOUT MONEY, AND SOWING AND REAPING

In addition, all scripture must be interpreted within the context of the verses before and after. For example, if the verses immediately preceding verse 9 are talking about money, and if the verses immediately following verse 9 are talking about money, *then it would be impossible to say that verse 9 is talking about anything other than money.* It would have to be understood within the context of the passage.

What makes this even more remarkable is that not just a few verses are devoted to finances, but two whole chapters are devoted to finances! **All of chapter 8 and chapter 9 exclusively deal with finances** -- the financial offerings to be collected among the believers, how the believers should give finances in a proper manner approved by God, and the financial increase that can be expected because of cheerful giving.

So, without a doubt, II Corinthians 8:9 is talking about material and financial riches. God wants you to be a prosperous believer, -- a rich believer, if you will. God had a whole lot more in mind than most believers have given Him credit for.

Now to have a greater appreciation for what this verse is saying it's important to have an understanding of what redemption was all about. Since this scripture plainly states that Jesus became poor for us, the question is, HOW did Jesus become poor for us? The answer is found in Galations 3:13, By being made a Curse for us!

REDEEMED FROM THE CURSE OF POVERTY

CHRIST HATH REDEEMED US FROM THE CURSE OF THE LAW, being made a curse FOR US: for it is written, Cursed is every one that hangeth on a tree: That the BLESSING OF ABRAHAM might come ON THE GENTILES through Jesus Christ; that we might receive the promise of the Spirit THROUGH FAITH...And if ye be Christ's then are ye Abraham's seed, and HEIRS ACCORDING TO THE PROMISE.
                                        - Galations 3: 13-14, 29

It's important to realize that we have been redeemed from the curse of the law, of which poverty is a part. Every curse that would fall upon God's people for their failure to observe all of His commandments fell upon Jesus at Calvary. Jesus became a curse for us. There is not any way any of us could fulfill all of the law, for "*all have sinned and come short of the glory of God*" (Romans 3:23).

The curse rightfully should fall upon us. But because of God's great love for us, Jesus came in our stead. He willingly substituted Himself in our place. And instead of the curse falling upon us, it fell upon Him. *This is called **The Great Exchange**.* No longer do we have to suffer the consequences of this curse. We are now heirs according to the promise, not according to the curse.

To understand what Galations 3: 13-14, 29 is saying, we need to realize what the curse of the law is. When the New Testament uses the phrase, "the law," generally it is referring to the first five books in the Bible, the Pentateuch. The "curse" of the law is recorded in Deuteronomy chapter 28. Look at the part of the curse that has to do with finances:

15 But it shall come to pass, if thou wilt not hearken unto the voice of the Lord thy God, to observe to do all his commandments and his statutes which I command thee this day; that all these <u>curses</u> **shall come upon thee, and overtake thee:**
16 Cursed shalt thou be in the city, and cursed shalt thou be in the field.
17 Cursed shall be thy basket and thy store.
38 Thou shalt carry much seed out into the field, and shalt gather but little in; for the locust shall consume it.
39 Thou shalt plant vineyards, and dress them, but shalt neither drink of the wine, nor gather the grapes; for the worms shall eat them.

40   Thou shalt have olive trees throughout all thy coasts, but thou shalt not anoint thyself with the oil; for thine olive shall cast his fruit.

42   All thy trees and fruit of thy land shall the locust consume.

43   The stranger that is within thee shall get up above thee very high; and thou shalt come down very low.

44   He shall lend to thee, and thou shalt not lend to him: he shall be the head, and thou shalt be the tail;

48   Therefore shalt thou serve thine enemies...in hunger, and in thirst, and in nakedness, and in want of all things..

51   And he shall eat the fruit of thy cattle, and the fruit of thy land, until thou be destroyed: which also shall not leave thee either corn, wine, or oil, or the increase of thy kine, or flocks of thy sheep...

- Deut. 28: 15-17, 38-40, 42-44, 48, 51

It's amazing to realize the full extent of this curse. Whether one was a businessman in the city, or a farmer in the field, his every endeavor was under a curse (v. 16). His daily needs (his basket) and his long range savings (his store) were under a curse. Regardless of how large his profit potential appeared, he would bring but a little in (v. 38). And according to verses 38, 39, and 40, no matter how many hours he put in each day, it all turned to nil. In fact, verse 42 states that everything he possessed would be lost.

Then, to add insult to injury, verses 43 and 44 make it clear that foreign interest would gain the mastery over him and his business. Business and personal loans would go bad, and instead of being in control, he would end up being controlled. His enemies would move in, buy-outs would take place, bankruptcies would occur, and all possessions would be lost.

57

Without any doubt, poverty is a curse. Though this curse should rightfully fall upon us, instead, thanks be to God, Christ redeemed us from the curse of the law. The curse fell upon Jesus at Calvary's cross.

How was this done? *In the same way that sin and sickness was placed on Him.* You see, II Corinthians 5:21 states that Jesus was made to be sin for us, and Matthew 8:17 states that Jesus took our infirmities and bare our sicknesses.

This doesn't mean, though, that Jesus lived 33 years of a sinful life, and neither does it mean He lived 33 years of sickness and disease. Contrariwise, Jesus was the epitome of righteousness and holiness, and He was likewise the epitome of health, vitality, and life. He was the Master over sin, sickness, and disease.

But when He willingly gave Himself up as the sacrificial lamb, the CAUSE of sin, sickness, and disease was placed on Him. HE WAS MADE A CURSE FOR US! -- "Cursed is every one that hangeth on a tree" (Galations 3:13).

Likewise, when Jesus came to the earth He didn't live 33 years of poverty and lack. He was the Master over poverty. When 5,000 men unexpectedly showed (not counting women and children), He was more than able to provide for their immediate needs. When those who received the tribute money showed for collection, He was immediately able to provide the necessary money from a fish's mouth. When He wanted to bless the poor with finances He just simply opened his money bag (John 13:29). *Everything about Jesus portrayed abundance,* even in His choice of clothing.

But when the appointed time came, when He willingly gave Himself as the sacrificial lamb, the CAUSE of poverty was placed on Jesus. *JESUS BECAME POOR FOR US BY BEING MADE A CURSE FOR US.* We have been totally and completely set free. For what purpose?

That the blessing of Abraham might come ON THE GENTILES THROUGH JESUS CHRIST...
- Galations 3:14

This is you and me the apostle Paul is writing about. The blessing of God that Abraham enjoyed (see chapter 3) has been made available to us through Jesus Christ. This is not for just the *physical* descendants of Abraham. Again, look at Galations 3:29:

And if ye be Christ's, THEN ARE YE ABRAHAM'S SEED, AND HEIRS ACCORDING TO THE PROMISE.
- Galations 3:29

If Jesus is our Lord and Savior, we, too, are Abraham's seed, as well as heirs. We have been redeemed from the curse of the law, and are now able to partake of the same blessings God offered the children of Israel in Deuteronomy 28: 1-13. Notice:

GOD'S BLESSINGS OF PROSPERITY

3 Blessed shalt thou be in the city, and blessed shalt thou be in the field.
4 Blessed shall be the fruit of thy body, and the fruit of thy ground, and the fruit of thy cattle, the increase of thy kine, and the flocks of thy sheep.
5 Blessed shall be thy basket and thy store.
6 Blessed shalt thou be when thou comest in, and blessed shalt thou be when thou goest out.

7 The LORD shall cause thine enemies that rise up against thee to be smitten before thy face: they shall come out against thee one way, and flee before thee seven ways.

8 The LORD shall command the BLESSING upon thee in thy storehouses (savings accounts), and in all that thou settest thine hand unto; and he shall BLESS thee in the land which the LORD thy God giveth thee.

11 And the LORD shall make thee plenteous in goods, in the fruit of thy body, and in the fruit of thy cattle, and in the fruit of thy ground...

12 The LORD shall open unto thee his GOOD TREASURE, the heaven to give the rain unto thy land in his season, and to BLESS all the work of thine hand: and thou shalt lend unto many nations, and thou shalt not borrow.

13 And the LORD shall make thee the head, and not the tail; and thou shalt be above ONLY, and thou shalt not be beneath...

- Deuteronomy 28: 3-8, 11-13

As can plainly be seen, financial prosperity is a *blessing*, and it is the will of God for *every* child of God. *Not one time was poverty ever called a blessing by God, it was always called a curse.* When Jesus went to the cross on Golgotha's hill, He not only redeemed us from the curse of Sin, He not only redeemed us from the curse of sickness and disease, He also redeemed us from the curse of poverty. The Prosperity that Man lost at the Fall was regained at Calvary.

DOES GOD MEET ONLY OUR NEEDS?

NEEDS

VS.

ABUNDANCE

(a continuing study on financial prosperity being the will of God)

Introduction to Section 2

As can be seen from the individuals in Section 1, God did a whole lot more in their lives than to just supply their needs. _God gave them extreme wealth._ Yet the thinking by many in the Church has been the persistent belief that God is only interested in meeting people's needs. Many of these people have been very sincere, very holy, and very good people. And I would never question their sincerity, nor their holiness, nor their good moral conduct. I only question the erroneous doctrine that has been handed down century after century in many of our churches.

God most definitely does not want us to just barely get by. Television time for the gospel can't be bought by people who are just barely getting by. Billions of witnessing tracts can't be bought by people who are just barely getting by. Nation-reaching crusades can't be held by people who are just barely getting by. God _wants_ His people to experience financial abundance. But what about Philippians 4:19? David certainly experienced finances beyond Philippians 4:19. So did Solomon. So did Joseph of Arimathea. So did Abraham. And many others. Let's continue this study to prove _from the scriptures_ that God wants us to **prosper.**

CHAPTER
6

PHILIPPIANS 4:19

But my God shall supply all your need according to his riches in glory by Christ Jesus.

- Philippians 4:19

Some Christians think that God is only interested in meeting our needs. But II Corinthians 9:8 quickly dispels this notion:

God is able to make it up to you by giving you everything you need AND MORE, so that there will not only be enough for your own needs, BUT PLENTY LEFT OVER to give joyfully to others.

- II Corinthians 9:8, The Living Bible

God wants to meet our needs _and more_, with _plenty left over._ Some people think they're being humble when they make statements like, "_I only want enough for me and my family._" But really, statements like this are not humble, it's ignorance of God's Word. This is the result of either small thinking, selfishness, or just plain ignorance.

63

If, for example, we only have enough to get by, that means we don't have anything extra to give to someone who is hurting, or to the poor, or for the work of the ministry. There are so many hurting people, there are so many needs that have to be met, and there are so many people who have never heard the good news of our Lord Jesus Christ that, actually, it's almost criminal to think in terms of only getting enough for ourselves.

I find it interesting what God said to Abraham:

...and I WILL BLESS THEE... and THOU SHALT BE A BLESSING;

- Genesis 12:2

In other words, God said that He was going to bless Abraham and then, in turn, Abraham would be a blessing. You see, we can't _be_ a blessing _until we've first been blessed._ Neither can we help others if we haven't first been helped. But if, as II Corinthians 9:8 states, we have everything we need AND MORE, we can then be a part of the answer instead of being a part of the problem.

But what about Philippians 4:19? Is this, in fact, telling us that God is only interested in meeting our needs? _This answer is an easy no._ II Corinthians 9:8 easily disproves this.

...ACCORDING TO HIS RICHES IN HEAVEN

The key to understanding Phillipians 4:19 is in reading the whole verse, not just the first half of it. You'll notice it doesn't read, _"My God shall supply all your need."_ Instead, it reads, _"My God shall supply all your need ACCORDING TO."_ This is a big difference. Notice:

64

PHILIPPIANS 4:19

But my God shall supply all your need ACCORDING TO HIS RICHES IN GLORY by Christ Jesus.
- Philippians 4:19

The key phrase in this verse is, "*according to his riches in glory.*" Let me give you an example -- Suppose I was the son of John D. Rockefeller, who in his day was the richest man in the world, a multi-billionaire. And as his son, my every need would be supplied according to *his* riches. I ask you, would I suffer lack or want? Of course not.

Although my needs are the same as every other human being (For example -- I,too, would need a house, a car, clothes, etc.), yet my needs would be taken care of *in a way completely different than every other human being.* Why? **Because I would be the son of the richest man in the world.**

If my need is a house, what kind of a house would John D. Rockefeller provide me? It would obviously be the best house available. If my need is a car, what kind of a car would John D. Rockefeller provide me? It would obviously be the best car available. If my need is clothes, what kind of clothes would John D. Rockefeller provide me? Again, it would be the best clothes available.

You see, my needs wouldn't be supplied according to the limited funds of a poor man living on welfare. As much as he would like to take care of me, his funds would limit his ability in *how* he would take care of me. His choice in clothing, transportation, and housing would have to be something on an extremely low level. Clothing would be Goodwill, transportation would be the bus, and housing would be government funded.

65

But because I'm the son of John D. Rockefeller, my needs are not supplied according to the meager funds of a poor man, my needs are supplied according to the richest man on earth. These same basic needs of housing, clothing, and transportation are supplied at the highest level possible. *How my needs are supplied is based by the wealth and the willingness of my benefactor*.

I now remind the reader of the words of Jesus:

Ask, and it shall be given you ... For everyone that asketh receiveth ... Or what man is there of you, whom if his son ask bread, will he give him a stone? Or if he ask a fish, will he give him a serpent? If ye then, being evil, know how to give GOOD GIFTS unto your children, HOW MUCH MORE shall your Father which is in heaven give GOOD GIFTS to them that ask him...
- Matthew 7:7-11

In this passage Jesus is giving us further insight into the nature of God. He compares how we treat our children with how God treats His children. If our children want something to eat, would we even think of substituting a serpent or a rock for decent, digestable food? Of course not. We want to take care of our children in the best way we possibly can.

This is Jesus' point. If we want to take care of our children in the best way possible, would God's treatment of His children be any less? Of course not. Actually, Jesus is saying that there's not a human being on earth who can even come close to treating his children as good as God wants to treat His children. Look again:

If ye then, being evil, know how to give good gifts unto your children, HOW MUCH MORE shall your Father which is in heaven give good things to them that ask him.

- Matthew 7:11

HOW MUCH MORE! No matter how good we want to treat our children, God wants to treat us better. There's not even a comparison between how we want to treat our children compared with how God wants to treat His children. In addition, God gives *good* things. Notice:

...how much more shall your Father which is in heaven give GOOD THINGS to them that ask him.

- Matthew 7:11

God gives _good_ things to them that ask Him. If I ask God for a shirt, God doesn't give me just any shirt, He gives me a _good_ shirt. If I ask God for a car, He doesn't give me just any car, He gives me a _good_ car. If I ask God for a house, He doesn't give me just any house, He gives me a _good_ house.

And the good news is, John D. Rockefeller is not my father, _ALMIGHTY GOD, THE RICHEST PERSON IN THE UNIVERSE, THE CREATOR OF ALL GOLD AND SILVER, IS MY FATHER_. **And my God supplies all of my needs ACCORDING TO _HIS_ RICHES IN HEAVEN.**

HEAVEN'S RICHES

I think it's important at this point to take a look at what the Bible has revealed concerning God's riches in heaven. Heaven is a remarkable place. The homes God has prepared for His children are not log cabins, they're mansions! The streets are not concrete, the roads are gold!

67

The clearest description of what heaven is like is found in Revelation chapter 21. This whole chapter makes for some very exciting reading. Let's look at a couple of brief snippets. This should serve our purpose in our study of heaven's riches.

...and the street of the city was pure gold, as it were transparent glass.
- Revelation 21:21

Everything God does is one of excellence. **God made His holy city's Broadway with gold.** It's also possible that all of the streets are made with gold, because in verse 18 it's mentioned that the whole city is gold.

...and <u>THE CITY</u> was pure gold, like unto clear glass.
- Revelation 21:18

This suggests to me that everything within the city, all of the buildings, the structures, the roads, are gold. This will be quite the spectacle. Incidentally, this street is not *paved* with gold, it's *all* gold. The buildings are not *overlaid* with gold, they're *pure* gold. Also, since the city is 1,500 miles square (v.16), Broadway is approximately 1,500 miles in length. It's amazingly wonderful to think of just how much pure gold is used in this one street, and how many gold buildings and structures are in this 1,500 mile square city. How much money is this in gold alone?

Then, surrounding the city is a wall 216 feet high (v.17), and made up of 12 different foundations. Each foundation is made of a *different precious stone*, and each foundation is 18 feet in height.

1st foundation - jasper
2nd foundation - sapphire

3rd foundation - a chalcedony
4th foundation - an emerald
5th foundation - sardonyx
6th foundation - sardius
7th foundation - chrysolite
8th foundation - beryl
9th foundation - a topaz
10th foundation - a chrysoprasus
11th foundation - a jacinth
12th foundation - an amethyst

It might be of interest to the reader who is unfamiliar with these stones to at least have a brief description of each stone. The jasper stone is generally described as a green quartz, a very beautiful, expensive stone. Some commentators, though, believe this stone to be a diamond. Either way, this stone is a very extravagant stone.

This **first** foundation of jasper is 18 feet high, and runs east to west 1,500 miles in length, west to north 1,500 miles in length, north to east 1,500 miles in length, and east to south 1,500 miles in length, for a grand total of 6,000 miles of 18 feet high of jasper!! ($?)

The **second** foundation is sapphire, which is blue with gold specks, next to a diamond in hardness. Again, 6,000 miles in length, 18 feet high.

The **third** foundation is a chalcedony, a transparent stone which is sky-blue in color.

The **fourth** foundation is an emerald, a beryl which is a bright green.

The **fifth** foundation is sardonyx, an agate stone which is white with layers of red.

69

The **sixth** foundation is the sardius, a stone which is fiery red.

The **seventh** foundation is the chrysolyte, a stone the color of gold and yellow, a species of topaz.

The **eighth** foundation is the beryl, a transparent gem sea-green in color.

The **ninth** foundation is a topaz, a gem the color of golden green.

The **tenth** foundation is a chrysoprasus, a chrysolite kind of stone the color of blue-green.

The **eleventh** foundation is a jacinth, a stone the color of blue.

The **twelth** foundation is an amethyst, a stone the color of purple.

Each foundation is 18 feet in height, 6,000 miles in length. If you were in the countryside walking into the city I suppose it would look as if you were walking into a rainbow 6,000 miles long, 216 feet high! Then, in each of these four walls are three gates composed of solid pearl.

God's throne is described in Revelation 4:3, "*And he that sat (upon the throne) was to look upon like a jasper and a sardine (sardius) stone: and there was a rainbow round about the throne, in sight like unto an emerald.*" The throne room floor is described as, "*...a sea of glass*" (Rev. 4:6).

I trust the reader is getting a picture of what portions of heaven look like, as well as the incredibly exorbitant

70

cost to which these items would all add. It's almost difficult to imagine in monetary terms, but thanks be to God, it's all in the Book. These are the riches that we, His children, will be experiencing for all of eternity. The gold and the precious stones are not things locked away in a safe somewhere only to be used for special occasions. These are the things we'll walk on and be around.

It just comes down to the fact that we need to change our thinking. *What the world calls a luxury here on earth is just simply a part of daily life in heaven.* God hasn't spared any expense. And we need to learn to think the way God thinks. In fact, Jesus prayed, "*...thy will be done in earth (just) as it is in heaven*" (Matthew 6:10). In other words, just as God's will concerning prosperity is accomplished in heaven, God wants His prosperity accomplished in earth!!

A CLOSER LOOK AT PHILIPPIANS 4:19

But my God shall supply all your need ACCORDING TO his riches in glory by Christ Jesus.
- Philippians 4:19

The definition of the phrase "according to" in *The New Lexicon Webster's Encyclopedic Dictionary Of The English Language,* means, "*in a manner consistent with.*" Substituting this definition in the place of the phrase "according to," Philippians 4:19 reads like this:

But my God shall supply all your need *IN A MANNER CONSISTENT WITH* HIS RICHES IN GLORY (HEAVEN) by Christ Jesus.
- Philippians 4:19, author's priviledge

This confirms the fact that God doesn't want His children to live like paupers. God doesn't want to supply your

71

every need *based only on what you require to just barely get by.* God wants to take care of your needs here on earth *in a manner consistent with* what He enjoys in heaven.

When I'll need a house in heaven, what kind of a house will heaven supply? It will obviously be the best available.Thus, while I'm on the earth, though I can't yet have that heavenly house, I can have a house *in a manner consistent with* that heavenly house. In other words, God wants to supply my need for a house with the best house earth can supply.

When I'll need clothes in heaven, what kind of clothes will heaven supply? It will obviously be the best available. Thus, while I'm on the earth, though I can't yet wear those heavenly clothes, I can wear clothes *in a manner consistent with* those heavenly clothes. Again, God wants to supply my need for clothes with the best clothes earth can supply.

When I'll need a vehicle for transportation in heaven (if vehicles will be needed), what kind of transportation would heaven supply? It will obviously be the best available. Thus, while I'm on the earth, God wants to supply my need for transportation *in a manner consistent with* how heaven would supply it, i.e., the best vehicle earth can supply.

God's highest plan and deepest desire is that all of our needs here on earth would be supplied in a manner consistent with heaven's riches. God *wants* to take care of His children a whole lot better than most Christians have ever dreamed. This fits in beautifully with how the *Amplified Bible* translates this verse:

PHILIPPIANS 4:19

And my God will LIBERALLY supply (FILL TO THE FULL) your EVERY need...
- Philippians 4:19, *The Amplified Bible*

As can be seen, God is not in the business of trying to get by with His people as chintzy as He can. God is in the business of *liberally* supplying, and *filling to the full* our every need. Then, when the first half of this translation is combined with the dictionary definition of "according to," Philippians 4:19 reads like this:

And my God will LIBERALLY supply (FILL TO THE FULL) your EVERY need IN A MANNER CONSISTENT WITH HIS RICHES IN HEAVEN by Christ Jesus.
- Philippians 4:19

Again, God doesn't want you to *barely* get by, God wants you to *abundantly* succeed. Also, in addition to our needs being taken care of in a manner consistent with heaven's riches, *God wants us to have an abundance in our storehouses so that we can be a part of helping others and supporting the ministry.* Look at II Corinthians 9:8 again:

God is able to make it up to you by giving you everything you need AND MORE, so that there will not only be enough for your own needs, BUT PLENTY LEFT OVER to give joyfully to others.
- II Corinthians 9:8, *The Living Bible*

This is fully consistent with Deuteronomy 8:18, which says that God gives His people the power to get WEALTH to establish His covenant in the earth. The very nature of the word, "wealth," means, "an abundance, an overflow." Clearly, God is a God of abundance! And as can be seen, Philippians 4:19 cannot be used to talk against abundant prosperity, *it is all in favor of abundant prosperity!*

CHAPTER
7

ALL THESE THINGS SHALL BE ADDED UNTO YOU

For after ALL THESE THINGS do the Gentiles seek: for your heavenly Father knoweth that ye have need of ALL THESE THINGS.

But seek ye first the kingdom of God, and his righteousness; and ALL THESE THINGS shall be added unto you.

- Matthew 6:32-33

If we're seeking first the kingdom of God and His righteousness, there is nothing wrong with all of these things being added unto us. The question is, though, what are *all these things* Jesus is talking about?

In verses 25 through 31 Jesus is telling us not to worry about what we're going to eat, what we're going to drink, and what we're going to wear. In other words, Jesus is telling us not to worry about the *basic necessities of life*. God knows we need food and drink, God knows we need to have clothes, God knows we need a house, and God knows we need a car, etc. Then, after all of this is stated, is when verse 32 enters the picture, *"For after all these things do the Gentiles seek: for your heavenly Father knoweth that ye have need of all these things."*

The better question is, though, to what _extent_ does God supply what we have need of? I mean, obviously, God **knows** we have to eat, He **knows** we have to wear clothes, He **knows** we have to have a house, He **knows** we have to have a car, _but the question is_, what **kind** of clothes does He want us to wear, what **kind** of food does He want us to eat, what **kind** of a house does He want us to live in, and what **kind** of a car does He want us to drive?

For example, if the world is driving brand new automobiles, does God want us Christians to drive old, out of date cars? If the men of the world are wearing double-breasted suits and silk ties, does God want our Christian men to wear second rate suits? If the women of the world are wearing stylish skirts and fashionable jackets, does God want our Christian women to wear out of style dresses and shoes?

To some people, these kinds of questions sound silly, but reality dictates these kinds of questions _have_ to be answered. That until they are answered there are going to be a whole lot of Christians who are going to settle for something other than what's best. _What is the QUALITY of these things that Jesus said God wants to add to our lives?_ The answer is found is verse 32. Look again:

For after all these things do the <u>GENTILES</u> seek...
- Matthew 6:32

The key word in this verse is the word, "_Gentiles._" What is a Gentile? A Gentile is _an unbeliever, someone who doesn't have a relationship with God, a person of the world_, so to speak. Thus, what Jesus is saying is:

For after all these things do <u>UNBELIEVERS</u> seek...
- Matthew 6:32, author's priviledge

76

ALL THESE THINGS...

Then, the word "*seek*" means, "*to try to get, an all-consuming desire.*" So this verse could read like this:

For after all these things do the *unbelievers* spend their whole lives trying to get.
- Matthew 6:32, author's priviledge

THE THINGS UNBELIEVERS SEEK

I ask you, what kinds of things do the people of the world -- unbelievers, that is -- spend their whole lives trying to get? They're certainly trying to get houses, clothes, cars, furniture, lands, etc. The better question is, though, what _kind_ of houses are the people of the world trying to get? What _kind_ of clothes do they want to wear? What _kind_ of cars do they want to drive? What _kind_ of furniture do they want in their homes?

For example, do the people of the world spend their whole lives trying to get the *el cheapo* furniture made from imitation, pressed wood? Of course not. They want the best of the best, the top of the line, the kind that is specially designed by a designer.

Do the people of the world spend their whole lives trying to get houses that are only 500 sq. feet big, in the roughest of neighborhoods? Of course not. They want the _finest_ of homes, the kind you can show off in the *Better Homes* magazines. They want their homes in the best of neighborhoods, with manicured yards and swimming pools, designer cabinets in the kitchen, in neighborhoods where people who appreciate the finer things live.

Do the people of the world spend their whole lives trying to obtain cars that already have over 200,000 miles on them? Cars that are so rusted out you can't even tell what color the paint job was? Cars with windows busted out that have plastic or cellophane taped over to keep the wind out? With interior so ripped you would have to sit on stuffing more than you could the actual seat itself? With engines so worn out you can hear them 3 blocks away? Of course not. Unbelievers spend their whole lives trying to get the nicest of cars, the best of the best. They want to get a *Lexus*, or a *Rolls Royce*, or a *Mercedes*, or a *BMW*. At the very least they want a *Lincoln* or a *Cadillac*. They want all the latest gizmos and gadgets, where the inside looks more like the Space Shuttle than a car, with interiors so plush you feel like you want someone to feed you grapes while you drive, ha!

If we'll be honest, we know these are the kinds of things that unbelievers spend their whole lives trying to get. In fact, whether or not they ever obtain these kinds of things is not the issue. The fact is, they all *wish* they could get these things, because Jesus plainly stated, "*After all these things do the unbelievers SEEK.*" With this in mind, look at what Jesus then said...

BELIEVERS CAN HAVE THESE SAME THINGS

For after all these things do the Gentiles seek: for your heavenly Father KNOWETH THAT YE...
- Matthew 6:32

At this point, Jesus shifts from the unbeliever to the believer. Jesus is now talking about you and me, *we* believers! Notice what He says about we believers:

For after all these things do the Gentiles seek: for your heavenly Father KNOWETH THAT YE (BELIEVERS) HAVE NEED OF ALL THESE THINGS.
- Matthew 6:32

78

What are all these things that Jesus said our heavenly Father knows we have need of? THE THINGS THAT THE UNBELIEVERS SPEND THEIR WHOLE LIVES TRYING TO GET! The good news is, according to Jesus, **God knows that we believers have need of the very same nice things the unbelievers spend their whole lives trying to get.** Verse 32 looks like this:

For after all these things do the UNBELIEVERS seek: for your heavenly Father KNOWETH THAT YE (BELIEVERS) HAVE NEED OF ALL THESE THINGS THE UNBELIEVERS SPEND THEIR WHOLE LIVES TRYING TO GET.

- Matthew 6:32, author's priviledge

God KNOWS that we need these things. God KNOWS that we need a *nice* car. God KNOWS that we need *nice* clothes. God KNOWS that we need a *nice* home. GOD IS NOT OPPOSED TO HIS PEOPLE HAVING NICE THINGS! God is opposed to people being covetous. But it's not the *things* that are the problem, it's the *attitude of the heart* that is the problem. This is why Jesus then added verse 33:

But seek ye first the kingdom of God, and his right-eousness; and all these things (that the Gentiles seek) shall be added unto you.

- Matthew 6:33

We can have the same nice things the Gentiles have IF we're seeking first the kingdom of God and his righteousness. *The difference is in the heart.* While the Gentiles are seeking the *things*, we Christians are seeking the kingdom of God and his righteousness. At this point in our discussion, the key word is "seek." Notice again:

For after all these things do the Gentiles SEEK...
- Matthew 6:32

But SEEK ye (believers) first the kingdom of God and his righteousness...
- Matthew 6:33

You see, we're *both* -- believers and unbelievers, that is -- *seeking* something. The difference is, we're seeking something they're not seeking, and they're seeking something we're not seeking. We both end up with the *things,* it's just that our priorities are a whole lot different than their priorities.

PRIORITIES

Their priority is to seek *first* the things, our priority is to seek *first* the kingdom of God and his righteousness. Whereas they want to consume their desires on their own lusts, our passion is to please God and be a part of getting the gospel to the whole world. Their motive is selfish and self-centered, our motive is to be a blessing to others. Their every waking moment is in pleasing themselves, our every moment is in delighting ourselves in the Lord.

This is precisely what Psalms 37:4 is all about:

Delight thyself in the Lord, and He shall give thee the desires of thine heart.
- Psalms 37:4

You see, #1) we delight ourselves in the Lord, THEN, #2) God gives us the desires of our hearts. This sounds exactly like what Jesus said in Matthew 6:33-- #1) Seek first the kingdom of God and his righteousness, <u>THEN,</u> #2) all these things the Gentiles seek shall be added unto you.

If our hearts are right with God, Jesus is saying, *"What things soever you desire, when you pray, believe that you receive them, and you shall have them"* (Mark 11:24). If our motives are pure, if our priorities are correct, Jesus is saying, *"And all things whatsoever you shall ask in prayer, believing, you shall receive"* (Matthew 21:22).

This is what brings glory to God. #1) We're living a "kingdom of God-first" type lifestyle, and #2) God is working in our lives in a supernatural way, i.e., we're getting answers to our prayers. Clearly, if we delight ourselves in the Lord, God is more that willing to give us the desires of our hearts. God doesn't have a problem with us having all of these things.

If the Gentiles are living in their dream houses, it's not right that Christians should have to live in tin-shacks.
If the Gentiles are driving nice cars, it's not right that Christians should have to drive a "rat-trap" of a car.
If the Gentiles are wearing nice clothes, it's not right that Christians should have to wear second-hand garbage.

Again, it is the will of God that we Christians have the same nice things the Gentiles have. The difference is, they spend their whole lives trying to get the things, we spend our whole lives living for God.

So, if your heart is right with God, there's nothing wrong with you driving a nice car, living in a nice house, and wearing nice clothes. God <u>WANTS</u> you to have all these things.

CHAPTER
8

THE POWER TO GET WEALTH

...for it is he (God) that giveth thee POWER TO GET WEALTH, that he may establish his covenant which he sware unto thy fathers...

- Deuteronomy 8:18

Lest there be any doubt that God is interested in meeting more than just our needs, Deuteronomy 8:18 is the clincher, the icing on the cake, so to speak. _God, far from being against wealth, is in the business of giving His people the power to get it._ Without a doubt, God does not want His people to be poor.

It wouldn't make any sense for God to give His people the power to get wealth, yet want them to remain poor. That would be paramount to saying that God gives people the power to get saved, yet He wants them to go to hell. No, if God gives people the power to get saved, that means it's His will for people to experience salvation. Likewise, if God gives His people the power to get wealth, that means it's His will for His people to experience wealth.

83

And if God wants His people to experience wealth, He certainly would want them to enjoy it. It wouldn't make any sense for God to want His people to experience wealth, yet not want them to enjoy that wealth. Again, that would be like saying God wants you to experience salvation, yet not want you to enjoy your salvation. That's contradictory.

I mean, if we give our children something from our own hands, we certainly want them to enjoy it. And God is no different. God does not want you to live in a 300 sq. foot home with a tin roof and drive a green Pinto. Neither does He want you to eat dinner on a card table and sit on a metal, folding chair, nor sleep in a sleeping bag on a concrete floor. *God wants you to enjoy the wealth that He gives you the power to obtain.*

"ABILITY" TO GET WEALTH

The Hebrew word translated "*power*" in the King James version of the Bible can also be translated "*ability*."

for it is he that giveth thee the ABILITY to get wealth...
- Deuteronomy 8:18, author's priviledge

As can be seen, God gives His people the "*ability*" to get wealth. Unfortunately, this is where many of God's people have missed it. Many Christians don't think they have the ability to get wealth. Some have said, "*But I don't have a college education, so the only thing I can do is work at Taco Bell for the rest of my life.*"

But now, wait a minute, if you're saying words to that effect, you're basing the truth of God's Word by your own qualifications. I'm certainly not against being qualified, nor am I against education and natural ability. Those are tools in your arsenal you can use to better yourself. But if you

84

don't have any qualifications, if you don't have any natural ability, if you don't have an education, *God's Word is still true and Deuteronomy 8:18 is still a reality.* Incidentally, do you realize that over half of all millionaires do not have a college education? Just from a worldly, natural standpoint that should give you hope.

But it's important to realize, there's the *world's* way to make money, and then there's *God's* way to make money. The world says you have to have a pretty smile, or a killer instinct, or you have to know the right people. But if you know Jesus Christ as your Lord and Savior, God can *direct* you to the right people, and God can give you a *godly instinct* to make money. You don't have to do things that would make you violate your conscience. Besides, what is impossible with man is possible with God. God loves to take people who have no ability, no qualifications, and no education, and then give them the *ability* to become wealthy. And this is the key -- it's *His* ability that *He* bestows upon you so that you can now do what you could not do before.

The world may say you're going to have to work at *Taco Bell* the rest of your life, but God is telling you He wants you to own your own *Taco Bell* chain.

The world may say that you don't have the ability, but God is telling you that He has given you the ability.

It's important to realize that God not only anoints men and women to teach, preach, and to lay hands on the sick, God also anoints His people with the *power* to get wealth. It's also important to realize that Deuteronomy 8:18 does not say that God gives His people the power to *just get their needs met.* It plainly states that God gives His people the power to get *wealth,* which is an overflow.

It's important for God's people to get out of a "needs-met" mentality and develop a "wealthy" mentality, or an "abundance" mentality. One statement David said that is applicable here is found in the 23rd Psalm, "*...my cup runneth over.*" For years the Church has been asking God to fill their cups, and as a result, their own needs have been taken care of. But if the Church would ever use their faith for cups that are not just full, but for cups that are running over, they would not only have enough for their own needs *but they would have extra to help others.*

Instead of being "cup drinkers," we need to be "saucer drinkers." *Our cups should be so overflowing we have no choice but to be drinking out of our saucers.* We should be using our faith for the extra , an abundance, so that we can make a difference with those around us. And, as I stated earlier, the pipe that carries water to the thirsty can't help but get wet itself. If we'll be a pipe for God's finances to flow through, we can't help but get wet ourselves with financial blessings. We should never be content just to get our needs met. It's time for the Church to start planning for a wealth of abundance.

Again, while we're blessing others, God doesn't have a problem with us enjoying our prosperity. Let's look at some other blessings God *wants* His people to enjoy.

MATERIAL BLESSINGS GOD WANTS YOU TO ENJOY

...thou hast eaten and art full...
- Deuternomy 8:12

God wants your daily sustenance to be *satisfying*. He wants you to eat the **good** of the land. He doesn't want you to eat of the cornhusks as the prodigal son did. God wants you to enjoy appropriate nourishment that is good for the body. If we have need of fish or bread, God has given us His Word that just as our natural parents wouldn't give us a serpent or a stone, neither will God give us bad things. God wants us to enjoy good food.

...and hast built GOODLY HOUSES...
- Deuteronomy 8:12

Also, God doesn't have a problem with you living in a _good_ house. The children of Israel were in the process of leaving the wilderness behind them and taking possession of the promises of God, _and one of those promises was that they could live in **nice** houses._ The margin in my Bible says, "and hast built _fine_ homes." Therefore, you can live in a _fine_ home. Again, God doesn't have a problem with you living in a nice house. I mean, He's the one who first brought this up anyway, not *Remax*. It's important to realize that the message of prosperity certainly includes nice homes. Notice further:

...and hast built goodly houses AND DWELT THEREIN...
- Deuteronomy 8:12

Many people are working two jobs a day to obtain nice things. They work 8 hours at one job, then come home for 30 minutes to shower, and then work another 8 hours at another job. As a result, they have a nice house but, unfortunately, they don't have the opportunity to dwell in it. But the prosperity God offers doesn't have any sorrow associated with it. God has a way for you to not only HAVE a nice house, but to LIVE in that house.

...and when thy herds and thy flocks MULTIPLY...
- Deuteronomy 8:13

87

Even in King James English, anyone can see that this is talking about abundance. *"Multiplying"* is a term that means to *increase beyond addition.* As most everyone knows, to *add* something is referring to simple increase, but *multiplying* is to *compound* the increase, to *intensify* the increase to a much *greater* degree.

And God wants our herds and flocks to *multiply.* Of course, most people today are not farmers in this sense of how the children of Israel were living. So what this is referring to is our **substance** multiplying, our **possessions** multiplying, how we make our living multiplying.

> **...and thy silver and thy gold is multiplied...**
> **- Deuteronomy 8:13**

In addition, God wants your SILVER and GOLD to MULTIPLY. It makes sense to say that if God wants your silver and gold to multiply, *it would have to be His will for you to have silver and gold in the first place.* So #1) there is nothing wrong with you having silver and gold, and #2) there is nothing wrong with your silver and gold multiplying.

You see, extreme wealth doesn't frighten God. Extreme wealth frightens the devil. The devil knows that if the wealth of the sinner which is laid up for the just would ever change hands *from* the sinner *to* the just, then the spreading of the gospel is going to make some advancements, and the kingdom of darkness is going to shrink.

So the last thing the devil wants is for you to *have* silver and gold, and he certainly doesn't want what silver and gold you have to *multiply.* But realize this, **God** does want you to *have* silver and gold, and *God* does want your silver and gold to *multiply.*

THE POWER TO GET WEALTH

God only has two stipulations for you having and enjoying this kind of prosperity, #1) that you don't forget Him, and#2) you don't say that you got rich by your own ability. Notice:

...and all that thou hast is multiplied; then thine heart be lifted up, and thou FORGET the Lord thy God...And thou say in thine heart, MY POWER and the MIGHT OF MINE HAND hath gotten me this wealth."
- Deuteronomy 8:13,14,17

You see, if we forget God, and if we think our own ability is the key to our success, then we're not a candidate for God's prosperity, and we're not available for God's blessings on our finances. *The condition of our heart is more important than the condition of our bank account.* If we allow ourselves to be lifted in pride we can kiss this prosperity goodbye. We can only prosper materially and financially *as our soul prospers* (III John, v.2).

But if we'll keep our heart *right* with God, and if we'll *remember* the Lord our God, and if we'll realize that it's *His ability* that's the key to our success, then we're in a position to be blessed beyond our wildest imagination. Wealth is just simply a vehicle to bring about a God ordained cause. Then notice, after all of these bountiful blessings are listed, we come to verse 18:

But thou shalt REMEMBER the Lord thy God: for it is he that giveth thee power (ability) to get WEALTH, that he may ESTABLISH his covenant...
- Deuteronomy 8:18

God does not tell you to get rid of wealth in order to be in the covenant, but because you are in the covenant

89

God gives you the ability to OBTAIN wealth. According to God, wealth is _necessary_ to establish God's covenant in the earth. It is not a "necessary evil," it is a "necessary blessing!!!" Wealth is a necessary ingredient in bringing about God's plan for the earth, therefore God wants His people to get it, use it, and enjoy it.

STUMBLING BLOCKS TO PROSPERITY

PIECING TOGETHER THE PROSPERITY PUZZLE

SECTION 3

STUMBLING BLOCKS TO PROSPERITY

Introduction to Section 3

All things that God offers are free, and are willingly offered by God, yet what God offers is received *by faith.* Faith is the hand that receives from the hand of God. But man's arch-enemy, Satan, has made it his job to keep God's people out of the promised land of God's blessings. The devil does all that he can to put you down and to keep you down.

Of course, the devil and his demons do not have the necessary power to combat God successfully. Just by sheer numbers the angels outnumber the demons 2 to 1 (Revelation 12:4), *not even counting the power of God.* In fact, the devil doesn't even have the ability to stop God's blessings from being received by the *person* who believes.

Thus, the devil spends his time working on *people* to keep them from *believing*. **Our battle is a "believing battle.** Satan spends the bulk of his time trying to deceive and confuse God's people. If the devil can confuse the truth of God's Word *to keep it from being understood,* or better yet, to keep the truth of God's Word from ever being heard in the first place, then the devil has won the battle. Hosea 4:6 states, "*My people (God's people) are destroyed for lack of knowledge.*" So, knowledge, and the understanding of that knowledge, is the key to possessing the promises of God.

Having said this, certain scriptures have been used by the enemy as stumbling blocks to confuse the people of God. Certain statements by Jesus, or isolated scriptures not interpreted in light of the verses before or after, etc., have kept many of God's choicest saints from gaining ground. This section is devoted to kicking over these stumbling blocks, these misunderstood scriptures. If we can gain this insight by *rightly* dividing the word of God (II Timothy 2:15), nothing, absolutely nothing, can keep us from forging ahead and fulfilling the plan and purpose of God. God wants His people to prosper, and it's high time for these promises to be fulfilled.

CHAPTER
9

WHAT ABOUT THE RICH YOUNG RULER?

...there came one running, and kneeled to him, and asked him, Good Master, what shall I do that I may inherit eternal life?

- Mark 10:17

The fact that Jesus didn't tell the rich man of Arimathea, named Joseph, to get rid of his riches in order to be a disciple clearly shows us we don't have to get rid of our riches in order to be saved. So it couldn't be correct to single out the rich young ruler as our example, and say that everyone has to get rid of their savings accounts in order to follow Jesus. Being poor doesn't earn extra brownie points with God, and neither does being rich.

Unfortunately, some people in the Church world have taken the stand that because Jesus asked the rich young ruler to get rid of his riches, riches must be something that is bad. But simply put, money is an inanimate object, just as a stone or a table is an inanimate object. The object itself isn't the problem, it's the person _with_ the object that's the problem.

95

For example, an automobile can be used as a vehicle for transportation or it can be used as a get-away car for a bank robbery. A kitchen knife can be used to slice bread or it can be used to inflict a wound. A gun can be used to hunt a meal or it can be used to shoot an innocent person.

You see, the automobile, the knife, and the gun are not evil objects in themselves. It's the _person_ in control of these objects that determines whether these objects will be used for good or evil. If a good person is in control, these objects can be used to _help_ people and to serve a good function. If a morally corrupt person is in control of these objects, sadly, something evil could be the end result.

Likewise, money in the hands of a good person can do good things. Money in the hands of a bad person can do bad things. But is the solution to _not_ have money? Of course not, anymore than the solution would be to eliminate automobiles, kitchen knives, and guns.

The key is to teach the Church what Jesus taught -- Seek _first_ the kingdom of God and his righteousness, and all these things will be added unto you. So there's nothing wrong with all of these things being added unto us, **providing our priority is to seek first the kingdom of God and his righteousness.** If our priorities are correct, think what a great blessing riches and wealth can be to the world and the kingdom of God.

Evidently the reason Joseph of Arimathea could keep his riches, and the rich young ruler could not keep his riches had to do with **priorities.** The rich young ruler allowed his riches to keep him from being a disciple of Jesus, whereas Joseph of Arimathea didn't allow his riches

WHAT ABOUT THE RICH YOUNG RULER?

to keep him from serving God.

It's extremely critical to interpret Jesus' account of the rich young ruler with the _whole_ of the scriptures on the subject of prosperity. As we've noted earlier in this book, many of the most spiritual people of their time were also very rich. Abraham, the father of our faith, was very rich (Gen. 13:2). Isaac, the promised seed, was very rich (Gen 26:13). Jacob was very rich (Gen. 30:43). Joseph was second in command over Egypt, the strongest nation in the world at that time. Job was very rich (Job 1:3). David was rich. Uzziah was rich. Hezekiah was rich. Joseph of Arimathea was rich.

The point is, these men were very spiritual men, very godly men, some of whom were God's choicest leaders for their day, and as has also been pointed out, were also very rich and wealthy men. So it's extremely unfair to use the rich young ruler as the scapegoat, and use this young man as an example to talk against prosperity.

The plain fact is, his problem wasn't that he had riches, _his problem was that riches had him._ He chose _not_ to seek first the kingdom of God and his righteousness, he chose to seek first the riches of this world. As you can see, his priorities were out of line. As a result, he missed out on a once-in-an-eternity opportunity to be one of Jesus' _handpicked_ followers. Think of how few people of his day actually had the opportunity to have Jesus _look them in the eye_ and say, "_Come, follow me_"!!!!! He blew it by a mile.

ONE THING THE RICH YOUNG RULER LACKED

In the beginning of this narrative this young man asked Jesus a question:

...Good Master, what shall I do that I may inherit eternal life?
- rich young ruler, Mark 10:17

This young man was asking Jesus how to be saved. Take note of what Jesus replied:

ONE THING THOU LACKEST: go thy way, sell whatsoever thou hast, and give to the poor, and thou shalt have treasure in heaven: and come, take up the cross, and follow me.
- Jesus, Mark 10:21

Notice, there was only ONE THING that was keeping him from being saved. Yet, in this one verse THREE things are mentioned:

1. **sell what you have**
2. **give the proceeds to the poor**
3. **come, follow me**

So, what was the ONE thing that was keeping this young man from having eternal life? Can eternal life be inherited by liquidating all assets and by not owning any possessions? No, of course not. Then, can eternal life be inherited by giving everything you have to the poor? No again. Listen to what the apostle Paul said:

And though I bestow all my goods to feed the poor...IT PROFITETH ME NOTHING.
- I Corinthians 13:3

You see, as wonderful as it is to give to the poor, GIVING TO THE POOR WILL NOT OBTAIN SALVATION FOR YOU. Thus, the **ONE THING** this man lacked was not in selling all that he possessed, and it was not in giving all of his proceeds to the poor. *There's only ONE thing that will inherit eternal life, and that ONE thing is in **following Jesus***. This young man made a decision to *not* follow Jesus. Why? Because his priority in life was to seek first the *possessions* of life instead of seeking first the kingdom of God and his righteousness.

Jesus then made a statement that provoked an astonishing reply from his disciples. He said, *"How hard is it for them that have riches to enter the kingdom of God."* Notice the response of his disciples:

And the disciples were ASTONISHED at his words...
- Mark 10:24

Jesus then gave further insight on an often misunderstood statement. Notice his clarification:

...how hard is it for them that TRUST in riches to enter into the kingdom of God!
- Jesus, Mark 10:24

From Jesus' own lips, once and for all, He made it clear that it is NOT THE *HAVING* OF RICHES THAT KEEPS PEOPLE OUT OF HEAVEN, it is in THE *TRUSTING* OF RICHES THAT KEEPS PEOPLE OUT OF HEAVEN. The number one priority in life of people who trust in riches has been to make money, plain and simple. If Jesus came into their thinking, he was immediately pushed to the back of their minds and forced to take a back seat. *Money meant more to them than God.* Sadly, eternity has many, many rich people in hell.

But money didn't send them to hell, anymore than smoking or drinking would send them to hell. Hell is not a *money*-problem, it is a *heart*-problem. Jesus answered the

question of *why* this rich young ruler did not follow Him --
his trust was in his riches,

THE ASTONISHMENT OF THE DISCIPLES

Also, the astonishment of the disciples deserves a
closer look. *If the disciples were poor, as has often been
thought, why would they be astonished at Jesus' statement?* Wouldn't they have been *in favor* of what some today have thought Jesus said? I mean, if being poor is how
a person gets saved, wouldn't poor people consider this
an opportune time to voice their approval of Jesus' supposed words against prosperity? For example, wouldn't
they have said words to this effect? *"Yes, Jesus, it is hard
for people with riches to enter heaven. That's why it's easy
for us to go to heaven, we don't have any riches. Glory to
God, Jesus, having riches isn't a stumbling block to us,
we're poor."*

Wouldn't that be correct? Instead, though, what do we
see?

**And they were ASTONISHED *OUT OF MEASURE*,
saying among themselves, Who then can be saved?**
- Mark 10:26

Notice, instead of voicing their *approval* of what Jesus
said, they were *dismayed* at what Jesus said. The fact that
they were astonished OUT OF MEASURE makes me think
something entirely different about their finances. I mean,
it's one thing to be astonished, but it's quite another
thing to be astonished *out of measure*. Listen further:

**And they were astonished out of measure, saying
among themselves, WHO THEN CAN BE SAVED?**
- Mark 10:26

Clearly, this doesn't sound like something a financially poor person would say. This sounds like something a _rich_ person would say. To the person with an open mind, it doesn't look like their poverty was on their mind, *it appears their riches were on their mind.* Take note of the words "*Who then.*" They didn't ask how those _rich people_ could get saved, they asked how _anyone_ could get saved. Obviously, the disciples could not have been financially strapped individuals. This is not to suggest they were millionaires by using our terminology, but I think we can safely assume that they had at least been moderately successful in their respective fields of endeavor.

THE DISCIPLES WERE NOT POOR

The scriptures are not entirely silent concerning the financial affairs of some of the disciples. For example, Mark 1:16 brings out the fact that **Peter and Andrew** were professional fishermen.

It's interesting how some people tend to think of Galilee as being a hillbilly area of ignorant peasants. But this is far from being true. Galilee was a well populated, highly active commercial center. The Sea of Galilee was a rich fishing ground. Fish were caught and pickled, and the demand for these pickled fish came from all over the Roman Empire. Thus, *huge* quantities of fish had to be caught to meet this demand, and many, many young men, seeing the potential profit, seized the opportunity to become fishermen, if for nothing else, for the Roman export trade.

In addition, **James and John** also had a fishing business in this area. In fact, the scripture says that James and John had "_hired_" help:

...and they (James and John) left their father Zebedee in the ship with the HIRED SERVANTS...

- Mark 1:20

Notice that these servants were not volunteers, they were *hired*. In other words, the Zebedee family *paid* people to work *for them* so that *they* could make larger profits.

Matthew had been in the tax collection business. So we know he was very well off financially. In fact, after Jesus called Matthew to follow him, Luke 5:29 brings out the fact that Matthew threw Jesus a GREAT feast IN HIS OWN HOUSE, and many fellow publicans got to meet Jesus. The point is, great feasts cost great amounts of money.

As you can see, what little is revealed concerning the financial state of the disciples shows them to have been successful at what they did. Now you can understand their reaction when Jesus said it was hard for them with riches to enter heaven. They were astonished out of measure, not because they were poor, but because they had been successful. And their astonishment led Jesus to clarify what was said. Again, as Jesus said, *it was **not** the **having** of riches, it was the **trusting** in riches* that endangers a person's ability to make the right decision to follow Jesus.

Then lastly, we have to ask ourselves what Jesus' final words were on this matter. Did Jesus conclude all he had to say about the rich young ruler after verse 21? or verse 23? or verse 24? Of course not. His final summation is found in verses 29, 30, and 31:

...Verily I say unto you, There is no man that hath left house, or brethren, or sisters, or father, or mother, or wife, or children, or lands, for my sake, and the gospel's, but *he shall receive* A HUNDREDFOLD <u>NOW IN</u>

WHAT ABOUT THE RICH YOUNG RULER?

THIS TIME, houses, and brethren, and sisters, and mothers, and children, and lands, with persecutions; and in the world to come eternal life.

- Mark 10:29,30

This is difficult for some to grasp, but this doesn't make it any less true. _According to Jesus,_ the person who leaves everything _for the gospel's sake,_ will receive not just eternal life, _but a hundredfold of the very thing he gave up **now in this time**!!!_ This needs to be underscored in every Bible, NOW IN THIS TIME.

What is it that will happen now in this time? He shall RECEIVE A HUNDREDFOLD. How was he to receive a hundredfold? By first GIVING to the poor.

Now I ask the reader, _based on Jesus' own words,_ was Jesus telling this rich young ruler to give away all that he had to the poor, _and then himself be included among the poor?_ Was Jesus trying to get this rich young ruler to become a poor young subject? Was Jesus trying to get this rich young ruler to STAY poor? A THOUSAND TIMES NO! _According to Jesus' own words,_ this young man would have RECEIVED A HUNDREDFOLD. **THIS CANNOT BE IGNORED. _The context of the passage is that the end result would be a blessing so large he wouldn't have enough room to contain it all._** This sounds a whole lot like Luke 6:38 and Malachi 3:10. Again, the ultimate purpose was not for poverty, but for _increased prosperity._ It is impossible to use the rich young ruler to teach against prosperity. As can be seen from Jesus, Jesus is all for it.

SUMMARY

The key issue conecning this rich young ruler was his misplaced trust. This young man had made a point in

103

keeping the 10 commandments, and he did a great job with the exception of one, the first and most important one, *"Thou shalt have no other gods before me."* Jesus said another time, *"You cannot serve God and money"* (Matt. 6:24). Of course, He didn't say you cannot serve God and *have* money, He said you cannot serve God *AND serve money.* Jesus then went on to say in that very passage that if we'll serve God by seeking *first* the kingdom of God and his righteousness, then ALL THESE THINGS will be added unto us.

So God is not against us *having* riches, He's against us TRUSTING in riches. If God has our love, service, and trust *first*, then we can have money and riches *second.* The problem with this rich young ruler was that he had his priorities reversed. He wanted money and riches *first*, then he'd give God his love, service, and trust *second.*

Concerning this backward priority, Jesus gave an interesting analogy. Notice:

...how hard is it for them that trust in riches to enter into the kingdom of God! It is easier for a camel to go through the eye of a needle, than for a rich man to enter into the kingdom of God.
- Mark 10:24,25

James M. Freeman's book, *BIBLE MANNERS AND CUSTOMS*, reprinted 1972, has this to say about the eye of a needle:

There is supposed to be here a reference to a pro-verbial form of expression common in the Jewish schools, when one desired to express the idea of great difficulty or of impossibility. Lightfoot gives several quotations from the rabbis, where the difficulty is represented by the image of an elephant going through the eye of a needle.

Some writers, however, think that there is allusion in the text, not only to a proverbial form of speech, but also to a fact. They refer to the *low, narrow entrances* to Oriental houses, and to the difficulty a camel would experience in entering, *though even a camel might enter if he would take off his load and kneel down;* which may be considered a hint to rich men who would enter the kingdom of heaven.

A recent English writer says: "In Oriental cities there are in the large gates *small and very low apertures, called, metaphorically, 'needles'-eyes,'* just as we talk of certain windows as 'bulls'-eyes.' These entrances are too narrow for a camel to pass through them in the ordinary manner, or even if loaded. When a laden camel has to pass through one of these entrances *it kneels down, its load is removed, and then it shuffles through on its knees.* 'Yesterday,' writes Lady Duff Gordon from Cairo, 'I saw a camel go through the eye of a needle, namely, the low-arched door of an inclosure. *He must kneel, and bow his head to creep through; and thus the rich man must humble himself.'*" - Bible Animals, by the Rev. J.G. Wood, p. 243. (italics mine)

As noted above, the eye of a needle was not referring to a "sewing" needle as such, but rather to an Oriental (Middle Eastern) LOW, NARROW ENTRANCE. The way for a camel to enter was to unload its possessions and go through on its knees. Once it was through the entrance, **he could then stand and have his possessions restored.**

WHAT ABOUT THE RICH YOUNG RULER?

Jesus' point is this, because this rich young ruler's trust was in his riches, he was going to have to do something similar in nature to a camel going through the eye of a needle. This man was going to have to unload his possessions, humble himself, and go through on his knees. But often overlooked have been verses 29 and 30 -- once he was through, not only would his possessions have been restored, it would have been a hundredfold restoration.

The follow up question then is, does every rich person have to give up his riches to be saved? This answer is an easy no, _unless their trust is in their riches rather than in God._ The apostle Paul wrote to Timothy:

Charge them that are rich in this world, that they be not high-minded, nor trust in uncertain riches, but (trust) in the living God...
- I Timothy 6:17

You notice that Paul didn't tell Timothy to have the rich people give up their riches. Instead he told them to be humble and not to trust in them. Quite obviously, _this sounds exactly like what Jesus said._ But even if they were required to get rid of them, (which they are not. It's important to point out, this is the ONLY person the Bible ever records Jesus telling someone to get rid of their wealth.), but even if they were required to, the end result would be that they would not only get back what they gave up, but they would get them back _a hundredfold._

Again, the central key to this passage is the misplaced trust. Riches are uncertain, God is not. Some people think that they can buy their way into heaven. But Jesus made it clear -- salvation cannot be bought, salvation is received by _trusting_ in Jesus. Once our trust is in God, prosperity is unmistakably the will of God for ALL.

CHAPTER
10

WHAT ABOUT BEING CONTENT WITH FOOD AND RAIMENT?

...godliness with contentment is great gain. For we brought nothing into this world, and it is certain we can carry nothing out. And HAVING FOOD AND RAIMENT LET US THEREWITH BE CONTENT.

- 1 Timothy 6:6-8

Some people try to use this scripture to talk against prosperity. For example, they say, "*See, the apostle Paul said we should be content with just having food and raiment.*" But here's the problem with their mistaken understanding of this verse -- I then usually ask them, "*Do you live in a house or an apartment?*" When they answer yes, I then say, "*You'll have to move out of that house, because Paul didn't say to be content with food, raiment, and a house, he only said 'food and raiment.'*"

I mean, if we're going to follow their reasoning, they would be out of the will of God by living in a house or an apartment. Sometimes I ask a similar question, "*Do you have a car?*" When they answer yes, I again say, "*You'll have to get rid of that car and start walking everywhere, because Paul didn't say to be content with food, raiment, house, and a car, he only said 'food and raiment.'*"

Of course, anyone with half-sense would realize that Paul is not against you having a house and car. This scripture is talking about_an attitude._ Our attitude is completely different than the world's attitude. Our priorities are completely different than the world's priorities. For example, people in the world are never content. They always have to have more and more and more, again and again and again.

Clearly, this scripture is talking about _greed_, i.e. the **love** of money. He's not saying money is wrong, he's saying the **love** of money is wrong. By far, the majority of the rich got rich because of a greed, a love for money. Their friends became stepping stones, large sums of money illegally changed hands under the table, and the temptations and the lusts of the world became a part of their lives. Look at the very next verse:

...let us be therewith content. But THEY that will be rich fall into temptation and a snare, and into many foolish and hurtful lusts, which drown men in destruction and perdition. For the LOVE of money is the root of all evil:
- **1 Timothy 6:8-10**

First of all, notice the "THEY:"

...let US be therewith content. But THEY that will be rich...
- **1 Timothy 6:8,9**

Notice there's a distinction between US and THEY. It doesn't say "US that will be rich," but instead, "THEY that will be rich." The THEY is not US. You see, the rich people _of the world_ live by the_love_ of money. As a result, their greed blinds them to the reality of eternity. As Jesus

108

said, they know how to live and plan for today, but make no plan for eternity. Plain and simple, as Jesus said, they are fools (Luke 12:20).

But does this mean that God is against _His people_ becoming rich? _Not if it's done God's way._ You see, there is the world's way to make money, and then there is God's way to make money. And we _know_ that Paul couldn't have been against people in the _Church_ being rich, because look what else Paul said to Timothy a few verses later in this same chapter:

Charge them that are rich in this world that they be not high-minded, nor trust in uncertain riches, but in the living God, who giveth us richly all things to enjoy; that they do good, ready to distribute, willing to communicate; laying up for themselves a good foundation against the time to come, that they may lay hold on eternal life.
- 1 Timothy 6:17-19

Evidently, Timothy had some rich people in his church. And you notice, _Paul did not tell them to get rid of all their riches._ First of all, notice the word "in;"

Charge them that are rich IN this world...
- 1 Timothy 6:17

There is a difference between being rich **IN** this world and being the rich **OF** this world. As Jesus pointed out, _though we're **IN** this world we're not **OF** this world_ (John 17:11,14, 16,18). The rich OF this world, according to Paul in verses 3, 4, and 5 in this chapter, are proud, knowing nothing, but doting about questions and strifes of words, whereof cometh envy, strife, railings, evil surmisings, perverse disputings of men of corrupt minds, and destitute of the truth, supposing that gain is godliness.

You see, we in the Church don't suppose that gain is godliness and godliness is gain. We're just saying that if we're already godly, there's nothing wrong with having gain. God gives us the power to get wealth and riches to establish his covenant (Dt. 8:18).

Again, notice that Paul didn't tell the rich in the Church to get rid of their money. Obviously, if riches would send a person to hell Paul would have taken this opportunity to tell them to get rid of it. Instead, look at what Paul said to the rich:

#1) Don't be high-minded (v. 17). This sounds just like what Moses wrote in Deuteronomy 8:14. He said, *"Don't allow your heart to be lifted up when your silver and gold multiplies."* You notice that he's not against our silver and gold multiplying, He's against us allowing our heart to be lifted up. You see, pride and prosperity cannot occupy the same person at the same time. This is the world's problem. But God says that we (His people) can't have both. If we want God's prosperity, pride has to be kicked out. If pride is allowed to sneak back in, then God says there's not enough room for His prosperity to stay.

#2) Don't trust in uncertain riches, but in the living God (v. 17). Faith in anything but God leads to problems. This is why many millionaires jumped out of 40-story buildings in 1929. When the Market crashed so did their lives. Notice that Paul called them *uncertain* riches. Money is extremely unstable. It goes up one minute and down the next. But if your trust is in *Jehovah Jireh*, the God who supplies your every need, you won't faint or have a panic attack if the Stock Market goes down. You *know* that the same God who gave you the riches in the first place can do it again the second time. Money may change, but God never does.

#3) Be rich in good works, ready to distribute, and willing to communicate (i.e. give). Jesus said it's more blessed to give than to receive. The reason the Dead Sea is a dead sea is because it only receives and never becomes a channel. If we never become a channel that God can flow through to be a blessing to others, our lives will dry up or become a dead end. There's no guarantee from God that we'll keep our prosperity. Reaping is possible only because of sowing. Harvesting is possible only because of planting. And prosperity is possible only because of giving.

So, in dealing with the rich _who were a part of the Church,_ Paul gave some guidelines for keeping their priorities in check with the will of God. Again, money is not the problem, it's the _love_ of money that is the problem.

In fact, some poor people are just as guilty of the love of money (if not more so) than their rich counterparts. Many poor people are just as greedy and selfish when it comes to money and obtaining it. They love it, not because they have it, but because they want it more than they want God.

The good news is, to those of us who love God more than anything this world has to offer, to those of us who will keep our priorities in line with God's Word, and to those of us who seek first the kingdom of God and his righteousness, God has made it clear there is nothing wrong with riches being a part of our lives.

Again, Paul is not saying in this verse that God only wants us to have food and raiment and not live in a house. Deuteronomy 8:12 is proof of that. God *wants* us to live in nice houses. Paul is talking in this passage about the unending trap of trying to keep up with the Joneses, always seeking after the things of life instead of seeking after God. Our primary priority in life is to follow after righteousness, godliness, faith, love, patience, and meekness (v.11). The *things* will take care of themselves, the *priorities* have to be taken care of by *us.*

CHAPTER
11

WHAT ABOUT JESUS?
(WAS JESUS POOR?
AND DID JESUS OPERATE A
FINANCIALLY POOR MINISTRY?)

...And they say unto him, Shall we go and *BUY* TWO HUNDRED PENNYWORTH OF BREAD, and give them to eat?

- Mark 6:37

Many have thought Jesus was financially poor, both as a carpenter and as a minister. It's interesting the funny traditions the world and some in the Church have come up with. I've always been amazed why people believe some of the things they believe without any scriptural evidence to support their belief, or without fully searching the scriptures to see if what they heard preached was actually true or not. One reason Paul and Silas considered the people of Berea more noble than many others they preached to was because the Bereans searched the scriptures daily to see if what Paul and Silas were preaching was actually true. We would do well to follow their example.

PIECING TOGETHER THE PROSPERITY PUZZLE

Let's think this through for a moment, first about Jesus as a carpenter, and then secondly, about Jesus as a minister. As far as the scriptural record is concerned about Jesus as a carpenter the scriptures are silent. Nevertheless, we can piece a few things together to give us some insight.

When I picture Jesus as a young man in the carpentry shop, I cannot imagine Jesus being an incompetent carpenter. I cannot imagine Jesus putting his hands to a project and it not being the best work any carpenter could ever do. Jesus did, and does, demand excellence in every endeavor. He demanded it of the disciples and He demands it from us today. Therefore, quite frankly, I believe *Jesus was the best carpenter this planet ever produced.*

And I cannot believe that the best carpenter who ever walked this planet didn't have enough work to do to pay all of his bills. In our town (and I'm sure it's true in any town) people want the most capable workers to do the jobs they need done. In our town the best plumbers can't keep up with all the phone calls. The best contract- ors can't keep up with all the orders for houses to be built. The best electricians can't keep up with all the work. The best carpenters can't keep up with all the work. People want and demand excellence, and the workers who have excellence in their respective occupations are the ones who are making all the money. That's a fact of life.

It's the sloppy carpenters who don't have enough work to do. It's the sloppy electricians, the sloppy plumbers, the sloppy contractors who eventually stare at the phone waiting for it to ring. It's the sloppy workers who don't have enough money to pay all of their bills.

114

WHAT ABOUT JESUS?

And I know, good and well, Jesus was not a sloppy carpenter. I can't even begin to picture that. Jesus was the epitome of excellence. Therefore, I believe Jesus could not have been a carpenter living in financial straits. That's plain, everyday business sense and consumer demand that fits any time frame.

In addition, Deuteronomy 28:1,2 plainly states, "**...if thou shalt hearken diligently unto the voice of the Lord thy God, to observe and to do all his commandments which I command thee this day, that the Lord thy God will set thee on high above all nations of the earth; And all these blessings shall come on thee, and overtake thee...**".

Look at some of these blessings:

* **Blessed shalt thou be in the city...and in the field.**
* **Blessed shall be thy basket and thy store.**
* **Blessed shalt thou be when thou goest in (and) out.**
* **The Lord shall command the blessing upon thee in thy STOREHOUSES, and IN ALL THAT THOU SETTEST THINE HAND UNTO.**
* **And the Lord shall make thee plenteous in goods.**
* **The Lord shall open unto thee his GOOD TREASURE... and to bless all the work of thine hand.**
* **...and thou shalt not borrow.**
            (see Deut. 28: 1-14)

Now the question is, did Jesus hearken diligently to the voice of the Lord his God? Did Jesus observe and obey all of God's commandments? *Of course*, no question about it. *Therefore, God had to have blessed Jesus financially in every thing He set His hand to do.* Regardless of where Jesus set up shop, *his carpentry business had to have been a financial success.* God saw to it according to Deut. 28.

Now what about Jesus the minister? When Jesus began in the full-time ministry at approximately 30 years of age, He offered 12 men the opportunity to study under Him and to work **with** Him and **for** Him. Now do you realize how much it would cost _today_ to ask 12 grown men _to leave their jobs and to work for you?_ You would have to have a pretty decent business to be able to provide for 12 men an equal salary, or an equal share of the pie.

In addition, Peter was married and had a family to support. In fact, the people in that day married quite young, so it's easily conceivable that at least half of the disciples were married and had families of their own. Nevertheless, we know about Peter for sure. But not only that, Peter was also taking care of his mother-in-law.

So, as far as Jesus was concerned, there were some financial responsibilities involved on his part in asking these 12 men to leave their work and to follow him. 1 Timothy 5:8 tells us the man that won't financially support and take care of his family is worse than an infidel. _So do we honestly think that Jesus would have asked Peter to follow him, and have him leave his wife and mother-in-law to flounder around trying to make it as best as they could?_ Of course not. Jesus was the fulfillment of every jot and tittle in God's Word. Without a doubt, Jesus did not put these 12 men in a position of being worse than infidels when He asked them to follow Him.

Evidently then, _there had to have been some consid-erable sums of money that were going through Jesus' ministry._ To further prove this, notice the following:

...And they say unto him, Shall we go and *BUY* TWO HUNDRED PENNYWORTH OF BREAD, and give them to eat? **- Mark 6:37**

116

WHAT ABOUT JESUS?

The Greek word translated "*pennyworth*" is "*denarion,*" or "*denarius.*" As any Bible Dictionary will point out, a denarius was worth a day's wage for the ordinary working man in New Testament times. (Some Bibles will put a certain dollar amount in the margin which, generally, is an incorrect figure for our day. This figure varies from Bible to Bible, and from publishing date to publishing date. Obviously, a Bible first published a hundred years ago [reprintings carry the same figures as their hundred year old counterparts] will be different than publishings in more recent years. Economies change, dollars change, times change, etc.)

However, it's very easy to get a modern day figure. Since a denarius is a day's wage for the ordinary working man, we just simply find out what a day's wage for the ordinary working person is today. I realize, of course, this figure varies from city to city, and from state to state, but I think we can safely say that one day's wage for the ordinary working person is $100. That computes to $26,000 a year. Remember, this is for the *ordinary* working person.

We now have a way to figure out the equivalent of how much money Jesus was carrying with them. The disciples asked, "Shall we go <u>BUY</u> TWO HUNDRED **DENARION** OF BREAD?" Thus, 200 days' wages multiplied by $100 is $20,000. Now think about this, **Jesus' ministry team had the capability of purchasing $20,000 worth of food at a moments notice.** They didn't have to have an offering to raise the money, they could have left immediately to buy the food.

This leads into another fact -- we know that Jesus was going through some considerable sums of cash **because Jesus appointed Judas to be the treasurer.** Of course, a treasurer is not needed unless there's more money

117

coming in and going out than you can handle yourself. A treasurer is not needed to handle petty cash. Also, Judas was a thief (John 12:6). He was stealing from the treasury. Evidently he knew he could get away with embezzling funds, *because there was more than enough money coming in and going out to keep him from getting caught.*

So clearly, far from being poor, Jesus was dealing with large sums of money in his ministry. At that one time they had a minimum of $20,000. Really, they could have had a whole lot more, that's just the amount the disciples figured would be needed to feed 5,000 men, not counting women and children.

Also, Jesus wore the best and expected the best. When Jesus was anointed by the woman with the alabaster box of ointment, he allowed every dollar of that ointment to be used on his feet (John 12:3). In fact, this verse brings out the fact that it was "very costly." In verse 5 it says it was worth 300 pence.

Again, the Greek word translated "pence" is the word "denarius." As we've observed in this chapter, a denarius is the equivalent (at the time of this writing) of at least $100. Thus, 300 mulitiplied times $100 is $30,000!!! I would agree with the gospel writer, this ointment was a **very costly** ointment. And you notice that Jesus enjoyed every bit of it.

Judas got a little upset, though. He said that this ointment could have been sold, and the money given to the poor. It's interesting some of the things some people say. Some people get extremely upset if their church wants to put in a nice, expensive chandelier in the foyer of their building. They've said, *"Why, that money could have been used for the work of the gospel. It's a waste to use that money on a light."*

But listen to what Jesus said in reply, *"Leave her alone, she's done a GOOD work"* (Matthew 26:10). You see, in Jesus' thinking God was big enough to take care of the poor AND take care of the alabaster box of ointment. Likewise, God is big enough to take care of the work of the ministry AND take care of that expensive chandelier in the church foyer.

Quite frankly, I think we've just become accustomed for so long *from having to choose one over the other,* **instead of believing that God is big enough to take care of this one AND the other.** It just comes down to the fact that we need to change our thinking. We need to start thinking big and believing big.

Also, this verse brings out something else about the ministry of Jesus. Why would Judas bring up the subject of giving money to the poor (not that he was concerned about the poor [John 12:6]), but the fact that Judas was using this as an argument shows us that Jesus must have given money to the poor *on a consistent basis.* Another time, when Judas left Jesus to betray Him, the disciples assumed Judas had left to give more money to the poor (John 13:29). Evidently, being in charge of the money, there were many other times Judas had been sent by Jesus to give money to the poor.

Here's the point -- to be able to give, you first have to possess. You cannot give something you don't have. Incidentally, Jesus was not having Judas drop nickels and dimes into beggars cups. From our example in Mark 6:37, the disciples were ready to use the equivalent of $20,000 *on one occasion* to take care of the people's needs. Clearly, money wasn't even an issue. The disciples must have seen it happen over and over. Whenever Jesus planned to do something that required large amounts of money, the money was always there. Whether it was $20,000 for food or $30,000 for ointment, Jesus expected the best. *He freely allowed large sums of money to go out FROM Him, therefore large sums of money came TO Him.*

Further proof of Jesus' ministry team having money is found in John 4:8:

For his disciples were gone away unto the city to BUY meat.

- John 4:8

Some people tend to think that Jesus and his disciples sort of floated through life living on hand-outs, hand-me-downs, and second-hand items. Nothing could be further from the truth. Jesus didn't expect his 12 followers to go to the city to beg for food, and neither did He expect them to stand around until a raven brought them food. You notice that the disciples went to the city to BUY food, to PURCHASE food, to USE MONEY to obtain food.

And as far as second-hand items are concerned, Jesus wore *only* the best, not second-hand items. John 19:23 tells us his garment was without seam, woven from the top throughout. This can be confirmed by any Bible scholar (or even any secular history scholar), that *this garment Jesus wore was the very kind of a garment that was worn by the rich merchants and the kings of that day.*

Some people would call these *designer* clothes. They certainly weren't the kind of clothes sold by the modern day dime stores. Whatever tag you would want to put on them, Jesus' clothes were the best clothes available in that day. Jesus didn't wear the clothes of the common, everyday laborer, *Jesus wore the clothes of kings!* Because He was a king, He **lived** like a king, He **looked** like a king, and He **dressed** like a king. No doubt Jesus and his 12 followers dressed like the *ambassadors from heaven* they were. They talked the talk, they walked the walk, and they dressed the part.

The only scripture I have heard people using to say that Jesus was poor financially is when Jesus talked about the foxes having holes and the birds having nests, but the Son of man hath not where to lay his head (Luke 9:58). Obviously, this is a weak argument at best. As we've already seen, food, clothes, and large amounts of money were never an issue.

Besides, living as a traveling minister, *always on the go,* criss-crossing the country time and time again, what good would a house be to Him? He would never be able to stay in it. A fox and a bird stay in the same area, therefore they have need of a place to call home. They have baby foxes and baby birds that need shelter, protection, and security. *But Jesus was on the greatest mission any person had ever been given, and He only had approximately 3 1/2 years to complete it.*

A house would have been a hinderance to him. A house wasn't a commodity that would've held any value to Him. It was a necessity for Him to *always* be on the go. He *had* to reach the whole nation with his message. He said, "*I must preach the kingdom of God to other cities also: for therefore am I sent*" (Luke 4:43).

A *motel* would have been more of a use to Jesus than a house. But motels then were not available like motels are today. And the few they did have were in the cities. And, as His fame spread, large multitudes of people sought after Him to such a degree that even the cities were no longer accessible (Mark 1:45). His ministry required large, open spaces because of the huge crowds. Thus, even motels were out of the question.

People were the reason why Jesus came, and **people** were the reason why He lived and died. His ministry was a 3 1/2 year odyssey of changing the world. So did Jesus have a house? Maybe not, *but not because of poverty,* but because of a staggering ministry demand.

Yet even this can be challenged. When Jesus replied that He didn't have a place to lay his head *He was temporarily among the Samaritans*. And in Samaria, the reason He didn't have a place to lay His head was because the area had rejected Him (Luke 9:53). They didn't like the fact that He was headed to Jerusalem, so obviously, He had nowhere to stay while there.

But I find it interesting that when Jesus was beginning His 3 1/2 year ministry, *He apparently did have a house!* Shortly after He was baptized by John in the Jordan, two of John's disciples (one of which was Andrew, Peter's brother) came to Jesus and asked Him, "*Sir, where do you live?*" (John 1:38, *The Living Bible*). And Jesus replied, "Come and see." Then notice this:

They came and SAW WHERE HE DWELT, and ABODE WITH HIM THAT DAY...
                                                            - John 1:39

So, at one time, not only did Jesus have a house, it was evidently large enough to entertain guests! The fact is, before Jesus began the mission for which He came, *while he was a carpenter, he did have a house*. This cannot be denied. He may or may not have kept it while He was traveling, we don't know, the scriptures are silent. But no doubt as a young man working in the carpenter's shop He did have a house.

Incidentally, Jesus had a house while growing up with Joseph and Mary. Some people try to argue about Jesus being born in a stable, implying they were poor. But though Jesus was indeed born in a stable, *it was not because Joseph couldn't afford to stay in a motel.* It was because there were no motels with empty rooms (Luke 2:7). *Evidently Joseph could afford to stay in a motel.* How do we know? **Because he was looking for a motel room!**

Then, after Jesus was born, when the wise men came to see Him, Matthew 2:11 brings out the fact that the family had apparently moved into a house:

And when they were come INTO THE HOUSE they saw the young child with Mary, his mother, and fell down and worshiped him...
- Matthew 2:11

Then notice this:

And when they were come into the house they saw the young child with Mary, his mother, and fell down and worshiped him: and when they had OPENED THEIR TREASURES...
- Matthew 2:11

A gift from a king demonstrated two things -- #1) what the king thought of the individual he gave the gift to, and #2) what the individual who was given the gift would think of the king.

123

The fact that they fell down and worshiped Jesus revealed their devotion, respect, and loyalty to God, and to the One whom God had sent. Thus, **their treasures must have been gifts of opulent substance.** If there was any doubt about Jesus' financial condition growing up in Nazareth this should settle the matter.

SUMMARY

As we've noted in this chapter, the idea propagated by many that Jesus was financially poor as a child, or as a carpenter, or as a minister is a false concept. Just as Jesus was in complete command over sickness, demons, and the elements, so was Jesus also in complete command over money and money matters.

Jesus also had a heart for the poor. Because this world is under a curse, and until all things are restored, Jesus knew there would always be the poor. So Jesus made it a point to be a part of alleviating the needs of those God directed Him to. And as has been pointed out, you can't help the poor unless you're blessed yourself. Helping the poor wasn't a one-time thing for Jesus, it was His way of life, a lifestyle.

When money was needed, it was always there. They had enough money to feed 5,000 men, not counting women and children at a moment's notice. When the temple tax was being collected, Jesus had Peter pull the required money out of a fishes' mouth. Money came to Jesus through many channels, naturally and supernaturally. Many people even supported Jesus' ministry with their finances (Luke 8:2,3).

So was Jesus or His ministry financially poor? Not by a long shot. Jesus was "Prosperity Incarnate."

CHAPTER
12

3 MORE QUESTIONS ABOUT PROSPERITY

1. DOES PROSPERITY WORK IN THIRD WORLD COUNTRIES?

The general conception is that because third world countries are poor, the Bible message of prosperity can't work in those countries. Many people think that because the United States is a prosperous nation, only the United States can have prosperity preached to them. But this is akin to saying you can only preach divine healing to people who are healthy, and you can only preach salvation to people who are already saved. No, the people who need salvation preached to them *more* are the unsaved. And the people who need divine healing preached to them *more* are the sick. *And the people who need prosperity preached to them more are people and nations who are poor.*

PIECING TOGETHER THE PROSPERITY PUZZLE

Prosperity will most definitely work in third world countries. God's hand is not shortened that He can only work in certain countries. The only thing that limits God intervening in the lives of people is doubt and unbelief. But countries with money or countries without money are not a hindrance to God. He can work any kind of a miracle *if people will believe.*

Some people faint at what appears to be impossible situations. If they see a famine in certain countries in the third world they stagger at the promises of God. But I remind the reader of Romans 4:20. It says, "*Abraham staggered not at the promises of God through unbelief; but was strong in faith...*".

Israel, in the days of King Ahab, was suffering a 3 1/2 year dire famine, a famine to such a degree that Ahab was hoping that at least some animals might live if they could find any grass anywhere (1 Kings 18:5). But what was Elijah doing? He was enjoying the presence of God while ravens brought him food.

The country in Isaac's time was suffering a grievous famine, insomuch that all the inhabitants of the land fled the country. But not Isaac. In the midst of the most impossible situation, Isaac enjoyed his greatest increase of prosperity (Genesis 26:1-14).

The point is, the more difficult the situation, the greater the opportunity for God to work a miracle. The country or people suffering the most because of famine need the gospel preached to them all the more. It's not prosperity we preach, it's *Bible*-prosperity we preach. And Bible-prosperity doesn't cease to be true just because of the misfortune and poverty of certain peoples. Notice the following scripture:

> For the eyes of the Lord run to and fro **THROUGHOUT THE WHOLE EARTH, to** show himself strong **IN THE BEHALF OF THEM WHOSE HEART IS PERFECT TOWARD HIM.**
>
> **- II Chronicles 16:9**

God does not show himself strong financially only in countries that are prosperous, God shows himself strong to ANYONE, ANYWHERE, IN THE WHOLE EARTH, *if they will believe*. This is why we need to preach this message all the more to poor people and poor nations. One reason the United States is prosperous is because from our founding days, mistakes and all, we put God first in our lives. And even today, no other country in the world supports missionaries to the degree that we do.

Just as Isaac enjoyed prosperity in the midst of a famine, and just as Elijah enjoyed his needs being met in the midst of a famine, so can Bible-prosperity abound to anyone, anywhere. The Bible never changes, but people's thinking and believing will have to.

2. ISN'T MONEY EVIL?

For the LOVE of money is the root of all evil...
- 1 Timothy 6:10

This has already been answered many times throughout this book, so it's not necessary to go into a lot of detail here. Suffice it to be repeated briefly -- money is not evil, it's the LOVE of money that is the root of all evil. It's the covetousness for it, the unrestrained passion for it, the compulsive greed to obtain it that is the root of all evil.

But money itself is a necessity in our present world. Electric bills have to be paid with it. Phone bills have to be paid with it. Food has to be purchased with it. Clothes have to be bought with it. Cars, houses, lawn mowers, curling irons, shoes, chairs, garage doors, all have to be purchased with money. Money cannot be avoided.

In fact, there's nothing in the Bible that says it's wrong to want money. The Bible says it's wrong to want money *first*, above all else. God tells us our wants should be for the kingdom of God and his righteousness *first*. Then, and only then, can money be had. But what we seek after *first and foremost* is God and His ways. *Then,* all these other things can be obtained. So money is not wrong. Wanting money *above the kingdom of God and his righteousness is.* Money is necessary, and money is what takes the gospel all around the world.

3. Didn't Jesus say we would always have the poor with us?

Certainly we will always have the poor with us, but that doesn't mean that *you* have to be one of the poor. Look at Jesus' statement:

> **For ye have the poor with you always, and whensoever YE will YE may do THEM good...**
> **- Mark 14:7**

Notice the "YE" is not "THEM," and the "THEM" is not "YE" -- YE will be able to help THEM. Jesus didn't tell his disciples that *they* would be poor. He said *they* (his disciples) would be able to help *them* that were poor. The day is coming, when Jesus comes again, that poverty will be eliminated (thank God), and until that day, let us give much and preach much for the sake of the poor.

SECTION
4

GUIDELINES TO FINANCIAL PROSPERITY *GOD'S* WAY

PIECING TOGETHER THE PROSPERITY PUZZLE

SECTION 4

GUIDELINES TO FINANCIAL PROSPERITY *GOD'S* WAY

Introduction to Section 4

There cannot be any doubt that financial prosperity is the will of God for all of God's children. The scriptures presented in this book do not leave any doubt that this is so. God **wants** us to prosper. The three previous sections have been written to prove this point.

I honestly believe that in these last days God's people are going to experience a miracle of financial abundance. If some do not, it won't be because God is withholding it from them. It'll be because they haven't put themselves into a position to receive it. This is one reason why I've written this book. I want people to be ready. I want people to see from the scriptures that it's truly the will of God for them to prosper, and to prosper exceedingly.

But to receive from the hand of God there are certain conditions that have to be met. For example, are we a humble people? Are our priorities in check? Are our motives pure? Chapter 13 is written expressly for this purpose. We need to clean house, so to speak, in our hearts.

Following this chapter we get into the mechanics, the nuts and bolts, of what we can expect when we tithe and give offerings. Admittedly, some of the things shared in chapters 15, 16, and 17 will be new to some people. I think many questions, though, will be answered in these chapters as to why some people have never experienced the prosperity God has been offering. Added insight and further revelation is my deepest desire for the reader. I trust this section will bring illumination to your mind and spirit.

The question that has to be answered is, <u>HOW</u> is financial prosperity obtained? The material that will be presented in the following chapters hinges on our compliance with God's laws concerning tithes and offerings. We are either in a financial *curse* because of tithes and offerings, or we are financially *blessed* because of tithes and offerings. Thus, special attention must be placed on tithes and offerings if we are to succeed and experience abundance.

The wealth that's in the world was not put here for the unbelievers to enjoy. The wealth in the world was placed here *by God* for *His people* to enjoy. All the gold, the silver, the precious stones and gems go back to Genesis 1:1, -- "*In the beginning God **created**...*". This revelation is inescapable. <u>God</u> made all of these extremely valuable things. He made them with the express purpose for His family to enjoy. Too long has the devil and his children kept possession of what rightly belongs to us. It's high time for God's people to take back what the devil has stolen.

CHAPTER
13

PRIORITIES AND MOTIVES

But THOU SHALT REMEMBER THE LORD THY GOD: for it is he that giveth thee power to get wealth, that he may establish his covenant...

- Deuteronomy 8:18

Financial prosperity doesn't start with a raise at work, or by a new investment opportunity, or by a creative idea. Financial prosperity begins when motives are purified and when priorities are put in line with the Word of God and the will of God. God doesn't release financial increase until the heart is first fixed on things from above. Jesus plainly stated, *"You cannot serve God and mammon (money)"* (Matthew 6:24). Of course, He didn't say you cannot serve God and _have_ mammon, he said you cannot serve God and SERVE mammon. You can only have _one_ God.

By far, the majority of the scriptures that mention money and money matters deal with warnings about money. Money is very powerful and very enticing. Its allure can easily have a negative impact. Because money is something that is needed by everyone, everyone wants to have more of it. Money represents power. The more you have, the more you can do. As a result, some people are willing to do anything to get more of it -- lie, cheat, steal, and kill.

In a world that is governed by greed and selfishness, it's easy to be influenced by people who have wrong intentions, even evil intentions. Sadly, the majority of the wealth in the world is governed by the unsaved. Some got it by stealing from widows, conning the elderly, embezzling from companies, and blatant wicked schemes. Of course, some earned it the old fashioned way, by just plain old hard work, and for some, by being at the right place at the right time. And we thank God for those who are wealthy who have been a part of supporting the work of the ministry. But, by and large, these have been too few and too far between.

The day is coming, and now is, when God is looking for ALL of His people, not a few, to take hold of His Word and believe Him for wealth, _extreme_ wealth, to help get the gospel of the Lord Jesus Christ all around the world. It's high time for God's people to stretch their financial faith as far as they can stretch it. Creative ideas and financial opportunities are things God can work out in a matter of weeks, even days, but a person's heart is something that can take time to develop. As Deuteronomy 8:14,17 brings out, when prosperity comes to pass, will some people forget God and pridefully think it's their own ability that is bringing this wealth in? If so, they'll short circuit the very thing that got them to where they are. As Proverbs 16:18 states, "pride goeth before destruction."

So, the development of the spirit, as far as God is concerned, is of the utmost importance. Wealth is relatively easy to obtain, but the development of the soul and spirit to handle extreme wealth is something that needs to be incubated. A proper spiritual diet and a proper spiritual atmosphere that is conducive for spiritual growth is a necessity. A church home is a must. Hebrews 10:25 states, *"Not forsaking the assembling of ourselves togeth-*

134

er, *as the manner of some is; but exhorting one another: and so much the more, as ye see the day (of Christ's return) approaching.*" The person who won't stay plugged into a church is not available for this prosperity God is offering. Why? Because he won't stay situated long enough to mature in spiritual matters. As III John, v.2 brings out, we can only prosper materially and financially *as our souls prosper.*

Over and over the scriptures teach that before prosperity comes to us we must be seeking first the kingdom of God and his righteousness. Matthew 6:33 is as definitive as any scripture along this line. Our primary goal in life should be to grow spiritually by letting the kingdom of God and his righteousness grow and develop from within. Instead of seeking our own kingdom of personal ambition, we should be seeking the will of God for our lives -- How can I be more pleasing to Him? How can I fulfill His goals in my life better? What weights should I be laying aside so that I can run this race faster (Hebrews 12:1)?

I realize we're not perfect, and until Jesus comes again, no one will be perfect, but we can all be striving to mature in our walk with Him. We can all certainly be better today than we were yesterday, and we can be better tomorrow than we are today. Our ongoing emphasis should be to allow Him to work His ways in us.

Our hearts should be yearning to grow in faith. Our hearts should be yearning to see revival. Our hearts should be coveting earnestly the gifts of the Spirit (1 Corinthians 12:31, 13:1). Our hearts should be longing for the move of the Spirit. Our hearts should be longing for the teaching and preaching of God's Word. Our hearts should be yearning to study His Word in daily devotions.

135

Our hearts should be yearning to communicate with God through daily prayer.

The question that has to be answered is, what is the number one priority in our life? If we can honestly say *from our heart* that seeking the kingdom of God and his righteousness comes first, we're one step closer to enjoying God's prosperity.

PROSPERITY REQUIRES A HUMBLE HEART

Secondly, a humble and contrite spirit is required. The scripture plainly states that we are not to think of ourselves more highly than we ought to think (Romans 12:3). In Deuteronomy 8:2 is found an illuminating scripture:

And thou shalt remember all the way which the Lord thy God led thee these forty years in the wilderness, to HUMBLE thee, and to PROVE thee, to know what was in thine heart, whether thou wouldest keep his commandments, or no.

- Deuteronomy 8:2

The children of Israel were in the process of leaving 40 years of wilderness behind them. They were getting ready to inherit the promised land. That for which they had longed their whole life was getting ready to be fulfilled. And I find it extremely enlightening that before they could enjoy the promises of God they *first* had to be a *humble* people.

Pride and arrogance are a big hinderance to prosperity. The person who hasn't dealt with the pride issue is easily tempted to do foolish things with prosperity. An old proverb tells us a fool and his money are soon parted. A prideful person can fall into dumb money traps that a spiritually mature person would avoid. And God is not going to bring extreme wealth into the hands of a person who will spend it stupidly or lose it altogether.

A humble person will recognize that his ability to get wealth is really God's ability *on loan.* God has allowed him to be a steward of *His* ability to bring in finances that will further God's causes. As has amply been proven in earlier chapters, God is not against His people living nice and driving nice, but ultimately, God has a higher purpose than planes, trains, and automobiles. God wants this money funneled towards the expansion of the gospel. A humble person will recognize this.

MORALLY AND ETHICALLY BOUND

Thirdly, God wants people who are morally and ethically bound, people who are honest and full of integrity. *With God the end doesn't justify the means.* God does not approve of people who get involved in shady deals, or monetary dealings that ultimately hurt some people. God has much to say against people who use and abuse the poor. The poor are not to be walked on, and they're certainly not to be taken advantage of. The fact is, it's not that success is attained, it's *how* that success is attained.

God is concerned about the journey. This Christian walk is a daily walk. We are to *daily* take up our cross and follow Him. Thus, to ignore the basic principles taught in the Bible to achieve success and prosperity is condemned by God. The ten commandments were not done away with when Jesus came. Jesus plainly stated, "*I haven't come to do away with the law, I've simply come to fulfill it*" (Matthew 5:17). We are not excused from lying, stealing, coveting, etc. In fact, we've been given a higher command -- to love our neighbor as we love ourselves.

PIECING TOGETHER THE PROSPERITY PUZZLE

Some have said, "*But to be in big business you can't always do things by the Book. Sometimes you have to smudge a little here and there. Sometimes you have to be mean-spirited. Sometimes you have to do things that are unethical to achieve your goal.*" BUT I STRONGLY DISAGREE WITH THIS. Clearly, this is the reasoning of the world, not God. I'm not saying you should be a pushover. You can be firm, but God will not bless the man or woman who will do just "anything" to justify the end result.

Remember when it used to be a man was as good as his word, when a handshake or a verbal agreement was as strong as the Rock of Gibraltar? Yes, times have changed, and we have to be as wise as serpents, but we also have to be as harmless as doves. Certainly we're not to allow ourselves to be taken advantage of and to be easy prey for vultures. The point is, the person who lives by the Bible can be blessed by the God of the Bible. If it takes a miracle to get the job done, then God is in the business of working the miraculous in the financial realm just as He is in any other realm. Ethics and integrity are not opposed to extreme financial success.

PROSPERITY FOR THE SPREADING OF THE GOSPEL

Lastly, our highest priority, and our number one motive, should be the financial support for the spreading of the gospel all around the world. There is an interesting scripture found in Haggai 1:4:

Is it time for you, O ye, to dwell in your ceiled houses, and this house (the temple of God) lie waste?
- Haggai 1:4

First of all, as Deuteronomy 8:12 clearly brings out, God is all in favor of His people living in nice houses. God

138

is not against nice houses, He's all for them. But what God is against are the people who have nice homes, *but who don't do anything for the work of God.* **Haggai 1:4 is dealing with priorities.** There is so much work to be done. There are roughly 5 billion people that are in need of being reached with the gospel. It is criminal in the sight of God to live only for one's self and to ignore the greatest work facing the Christian.

It's interesting that God didn't have Haggai tell the people to move out of their nice homes. Instead, He had Haggai tell the people *to put the right emphasis on the right thing.* He wanted them to put the kingdom of God first in their lives. *He wanted them to put their resources focused on that which He considered most important.*

Then, it's equally important to notice that the people repented for having ignored the work of God. They then put first things first, they rebuilt the temple, and then the very next chapter foretells the coming glory of God and how the people of God could now enjoy God's blessings.

You see, when we seek first the kingdom of God and his righteousness, and open our finances for tithes and offerings, the kingdom of God advances, more people are reached, and we then enjoy the presence of God and the blessings of God.

Deuteronomy 8:18 states, "*...he (God) gives thee power to get wealth to underline establish his covenant...*". Nothing can be any plainer that this verse. Any priority other than this is sadly out of line and out of place. The *ESTABLISH-ING* of the covenant comes *first*, then everything else can fall in behind at second, third, fourth, etc. Therefore, we have no choice but to put our money towards the work of the ministry first. We support our church with our tithes, and support traveling ministers, missionaries, medical missions, Christian youth homes, rescue missions, food banks, music ministries, etc., with our offerings.

God isn't looking for people who have an ability to make money. In the right environment almost anyone can be trained to make money. Neither is God looking for people who have a *natural* ability to make money. No doubt some people from birth are more naturally inclined to make money, just as some people are more naturally inclined than others to throw a baseball. Money really isn't even the issue. God can give anyone the ability to bring in money. **The issue is the heart.** Who, like King David, has a heart towards God? Who is more concerned about the things of God than the things of man? Who is more concerned about pleasing God than they are about pleasing the fickle standards set by man?

God is looking for a people in these last days who have captured God's heart for a lost and dying world. God is looking for a people who are willing to see beyond their own four walls and reach out for a higher, stratospheric goal. God is looking for a people who will be so heavenly minded they can be a whole lot of earthly good. People with the right heart can be funnels for God to flow extreme wealth through their lives to get the needed and necessary finances into the hands of ministries with local, national, and international visions. *The heart that is right will have the right priorities and the right motives.*

CHAPTER
14

TITHES AND OFFERINGS BRING FINANCIAL BLESSING

8 Will a man rob God? Yet ye have robbed me. But ye say, Wherein have we robbed thee? In tithes and offerings.
9 Ye are cursed with a curse: for ye have robbed me...
- Malachi 3:8-9

Since failing to tithe and give offerings results in living under a curse, it would make sense to say **by beginning or resuming the tithe and the giving of offerings would result in coming out from the curse.** Thus, _tithing and giving offerings is God's way for man to enter the financial blessings of God and leave the financial curse behind._

So, for someone to say they can't afford to tithe and give offerings is a misnomer. Actually, people can't afford to _not_ tithe and give offerings. God has attached a long list of financial blessings for the person who does tithe and give offerings. Let's take a look at some of these blessings as listed here in Malachi chapter 3:

10 ...and prove me now herewith, saith the Lord of hosts, if I will not open you the windows of heaven, and pour you out a blessing, that there shall not be room enough to receive it.

11 And I will rebuke the devourer for your sakes, and he shall not destroy the fruits of your ground; neither shall your vine cast her fruit before the time in the field, saith the Lord of hosts.

12 And all nations shall call you blessed; for ye shall be a delightsome land, saith the Lord of hosts.

- Malachi 3:10-12

So it is the will of God that we should no longer be cursed with a curse (v.9), that the devourer would no longer destroy the fruits of our ground (v.11), that God's blessings in our life would be so large we wouldn't have enough room to contain them all (v.10), and that all nations would call us blessed (v.12). Obviously, God wants us to be out of the red and into the black.

As you can see, for a person to fight the message of prosperity he is, in effect, fighting the message of God Himself. It's _God_ who has made it clear He wants us to enjoy these blessings. It's _God_ who has unmistakably said He wants to rebuke Satan off of our finances. It's _God_ who's made it clear that if we support the work of the ministry first in our lives with our tithes and offerings He'll put our finances first on His priority list.

Let me make this as clear as I possibly can -- _God_ wants us to succeed and prosper financially. But God wants us to prioritize our finances for the support of the ministry _first_. If the support of His work comes first on _our_ list, our finances will come first on _His_ list. He even went so far as to say "prove me."

TITHES AND OFFERINGS BRING FINANCIAL BLESSING

...and <u>prove me now</u> herewith saith the Lord of hosts...
- Malachi 3:10

DEFINITIONS OF TERMINOLOGY

Before we go any farther it's necessary to establish some definitions to our terms "tithes and offerings."

1. TITHE. The very word "tithe" means "tenth." The Hebrew word is *ma'aser*, and according to *STRONG'S CONCORDANCE,* it simply means, <u>"a tenth."</u>

The Greek word is *dekatoo,* and according to *W.E. VINES Expository Dictionary*, also means, "a tenth."

To further clarify, in Genesis chapter 14, Abraham was returning home after his victory over the five kings (You'll remember that Abraham's nephew, Lot, had been captured). When he came face to face with the king and priest of Salem, Melchizedek, it records:

...and he (Abraham) gave him (Melchizedek) TITHES of all...
- Genesis 14:20

In the New Testament, the writer of Hebrews, in relating this same event says:

...Abraham gave a TENTH part of all...
- Hebrews 7:2

Without a doubt, *the tithe is a tenth of our earnings, one dime for each dollar.* For example, if you get paid $100, your tithe would be 100 dimes, or 10 dollars. If you get paid $500, your tithe would be 500 dimes, or 50 dollars. If you get paid $1,000, your tithe would be 1,000

143

dimes, or 100 dollars.

This should be a great encouragement to people when they're ready to return their tithes to God, whether their tithe is $10, $50, $100, or $1,000. That lump sum of money they hold in their hand to return to God *is only one dime out of each dollar.* And that tenth is going to be a part of allowing God to get involved in their finances in a miraculous way. That money is not "lost" money, that money is "miracle" money.

Let's look further. In addition to Abraham, we have the scriptural account of Jacob:

And Jacob vowed a vow, saying (to God)...of all that thou shalt give me I will surely give the TENTH unto thee.
- Genesis 28:20-22

Then, under the law as recorded by Moses, the tithe (which was already instituted with Abraham) was continued:

And all the TITHE of the land, whether of the seed of the land, or of the fruit of the tree, IS THE LORD'S.
- Leviticus 27:30

In the New Testament we have record of Jesus upholding the tithe. He taught that men ought to tithe:

Ye pay TITHE of mint and anise and cummin, and have omitted the weightier matters of the law, judgement, mercy, and faith: THESE OUGHT YE TO HAVE DONE, and not to leave the other undone.
- Matthew 23:23

Then, in the New Testament Church, the writer of Hebrews adds his stamp of verification on the tithe:

Here (on earth) men that die receive tithes; but there he (Jesus) receiveth them, of whom it is witnessed that he liveth.

- Hebrews 7:8

In this verse is an exciting truth -- when we tithe it might *appear* our tithe is being received by men, **but actually our tithe is being received by none other than Jesus Himself.** We also notice that tithing was not just for those under the Mosaic law. Abraham tithed 500 years *before* the law of Moses. Then, 35 years *after* the birth of the Church, the tithe was an integral part of the Church age. *Thus, the tithe has always been a part of God's plan -- pre-law, during the law, and post-law.*

In addition, it's observed that the tithe is a *set* percentage. The tithe is not something we decide on how much we'll participate in. It's not an amount *we* determine. The tithe is an amount that has been predetermined *by God.* *The tithe is always a fixed 10 percent* -- not 11%, or 15%, or 20%, etc. Money given beyond the 10% moves into the area the Bible calls *offerings.*

2. OFFERINGS.

...every man according as he purposeth in his heart, so let him give;

- II Corinthians 9:7

An offering is different than the tithe. The tithe is a **specified** amount, an offering is a **discretionary** amount. **The tithe is an amount set by *God,* an offering is an amount set by *us.***

An offering cannot be given until *after* the tithe has first been returned to God. An offering is what's given *in addition* to the tithe. For example, if a person is paid $500 at work, then the following Sunday in church he says he "gives" an offering of $30; in actuality, he's not done any such thing. He hasn't even tithed yet. Further, a tithe is not something "given," because the tithe already belongs to God:

And all the tithe of the land, whether of the seed of the land, or of the fruit of the tree, IS THE LORD'S:
- Leviticus 27:30

A tenth of all we earn *belongs to God.* It's not ours to keep or to play around with. And it's not ours to "give" to God, it's what we *return* to God, it *belongs* to God. **It's His.** In our example with the man who was paid $500, the tithe, which is $50, belongs to God. *After* the tithe the man then has the option of giving an offering of $30. And it will be blessed of God.

The scriptures refer to the tithe as something that is *paid*, or *taken*:

...the priesthood, have a commandment to TAKE tithes of the people...
- Hebrews 7:5

...(Levi) PAID tithes in Abraham.
- Hebrews 7:9

Ye PAY tithe...
- Mattew 23:23

TITHES AND OFFERINGS BRING FINANCIAL BLESSING

Whereas an offering is something that is _given:_

Every man as he purposeth in his heart, SO LET HIM GIVE...
                                        - II Corinthians 9:7

GIVE...for with the same measure ye mete (decide)...
                                        - Luke 6:38

Again, we cannot purpose in our heart _how much_ to tithe. Neither can we measure _how much to mete_ when we tithe. _The tithe is always a set 10 percent_, the tenth. An offering is an amount that we can decide how much we want to give -- small, medium, or large -- **after** we first tithe.

So, just as the tithe is not "lost" money, neither is an offering "lost" money. The apostle Paul had much to say concerning offerings. He referred to offerings as "seeds" we "sow" that, in return, causes financial increase, or harvest. (This is studied further in chapter 18.) Suffice it to say here, to not tithe and give offerings results in a financial curse. But when we tithe and give offerings it causes a financial increase. As the reader can see, we never just stay the same. We're either going backwards or forwards. **Tithes and offerings cause us to go forward.**

MALACHI 3:8-12

8 Will a man rob God? Yet ye have robbed me. But ye say, Wherein have we robbed thee? In tithes and offerings.

9 Ye are cursed with a curse: for ye have robbed me, even this whole nation.

10 Bring ye all the tithes into the storehouse, and prove me now herewith, saith the Lord of hosts, if I will not open you the windows of heaven, and pour you out a blessing, that there shall not be room enough to receive it.

11 And I will rebuke the devourer for your sakes, and he shall not destroy the fruits of your ground; neither shall your vine cast her fruit before the time in the field, saith the Lord of hosts.

12 And all nations shall call you blessed: for ye shall be a delightsome land, saith the Lord of hosts.

CHAPTER
15

TITHES AND OFFERINGS BRING MONEY-MAKING IDEAS FROM GOD

Once a person becomes a tither and a giver, the biggest question that has to be answered is _how_ does prosperity come? For example, if a person is in a job earning $30,000 a year, how does this person get to $50,000, $75,000, $100,000, etc.?

I think one of the biggest mistakes by many Christians has been to assume that because they are givers, somehow God will just make money increase. Or, all of a sudden, they'll be offered a job making twice the amount of money they're making now. Though this can and does happen, this is sometimes unrealistic. I mean, if a person is a kindergarten teacher making $30,000 a year, I don't know of any other kindergarten jobs offering $75,000 a year. Some jobs just seem to have a built-in financial ceiling. I don't know of any janitorial positions offering $100,000 salaries. High salary jobs are designated for people who've had 6 and 8 year college educations, such as doctors, lawyers, etc. So, if you're 42 years old, no law or medical aptitude, and no opportunity to go back to college, are you forced to work a job that will never help you realize your life's dreams? The good news is, NO, _if you tithe and give offerings._ Yet how does financial increase come? How is it possible to get out of a financial rut and succeed financially? The answer is found in Malachi 3:10:

149

...I will open you the windows of heaven, and pour you out a blessing, that there shall not be room enough to receive it.

- Malachi 3:10

The key word at this point in our discussion is the word "blessing." Notice again:

...I will open you the windows of heaven, and pour you out a BLESSING...

- Malachi 3:10

This word "blessing," according to *Strong's Concordance*, can also be translated "benediction." As such it reads like this:

...I will open you the windows of heaven, and pour you out a BENEDICTION...

- Malachi 3:10 (author's privilege)

In fact, the French translation of the Bible reads this very way. Let's examine this. The word "benediction" is a composite of two parts --1) bene, and 2) diction. "Bene" simply means "good." "Diction" means "spoken word." When combined it means **"*good spoken word.*"** By substituting this definition in the place of "blessing," or "benediction," Malachi 3:10 reads like this:

...I will open you the windows of heaven, and pour you out a GOOD SPOKEN WORD...

- Malachi 3:10 (author's privilege)

UNDERSTAND THIS -- this verse is saying that when we enter a lifestyle of tithing and giving God will then open the windows of heaven **and drop a good spoken word into our spirits.** When acted upon, these **good spo-**

150

ken words, or **IDEAS**, will cause a financial increase that is so large we won't have room enough to contain it all.

This is an extremely exciting revelation. Personally, I think this answers a number of questions as to why many Christians never prospered financially, *even though they were tithers and givers*. Many Christians have mistakenly had the idea that more and more money would just start coming in *without their having to do anything other than what they were already doing.* If they were working at *Taco Bell* when they became tithers and givers, because of a lack of understanding about Malachi 3:10, they never heard what God was saying to their spirit, and 10 years later they found themselves still working at *Taco Bell* with very little financial increase.

It's important to realize that God doesn't drop gold chunks from heaven into our backyards. Neither does He create millions of dollars to miraculously show up in our checking accounts. That would make God a counterfeiter. Think back to Deuteronomy 8:18 again. It tells us that God gives us the power to **GET** wealth:

...for it is he (God) that giveth thee power to GET wealth...
- Deuteronomy 8:18

You see, God gives us the ability to "get" wealth, to "obtain" wealth. By not understanding this, many Christians have continued at jobs less than ideal financially, and then wondered why Malachi 3:10 never seemed real to them. I'm guessing they must have been unrealistically waiting for ravens to bring them money, or similar type things, because they obviously knew that large sums of money would never come through their jobs.

151

UNDERSTAND THIS ALSO -- The money that we need is not going to come from heaven. The _help_ will come from heaven, but not the _money_. The money that God is going to bring our way _is already in the earth_. (The day is coming _when we are in heaven_ that God will meet our needs _with_ His riches. But for the present, God will meet our needs here on earth _in a manner consistent with_ His riches in heaven. But the money we need _now is here on earth._) And God will give us the power to **GET** that wealth already here on earth.

What is this power, also translated ability, that God is going to give us to get this wealth?   **GOOD SPOKEN WORDS!** Simply put, **IDEAS.** God gives the tither/giver _ideas_ to get wealth, wealth that is so overflowing we don't have room enough to contain it all. Let's look at a few scriptural examples.

JACOB

Jacob's prosperity began when he got an idea from God. Previous to this God-given idea, Jacob had to get along as best he could, and it wasn't easy. His father-in-law, Laban, was a swindler. In fact, within a 7-year period Laban changed Jacob's wages 10 times! Every time Jacob would start to get ahead and do well, Laban would change the way Jacob would receive his wages. Needless to say, it was a very frustrating time for Jacob.

But everything changed when Jacob received his _good spoken word_, his _idea_ from God. Notice:

And at the mating season, I had a DREAM, and saw that the he-goats mating with the flock were streaked, speckled, and mottled. Then, IN MY DREAM, the Angel of God called to me and TOLD ME that I should mate

the white nanny goats with streaked, speckled, and mottled he-goats...(The Angel said), 'I am the God you met at Bethel,' he continued, 'the place where you anointed the pillar AND MADE A VOW TO SERVE ME.
- Genesis 31:10-13, *The Living Bible*

Notice this -- *God gave Jacob this dream* **to prosper** *because of a vow Jacob made to serve God.* What was this vow?

And Jacob VOWED A VOW, saying, If God will be with me...then shall the Lord be my God...and of all that thou shalt give me I WILL SURELY GIVE THE TENTH UNTO THEE.   - Genesis 28:20-22

This dream to prosper was given to Jacob in direct response to his vow to tithe of all that God gave him. This cannot be overlooked. Jacob was given supernatural guidance to prosper, a financial dream, a good spoken word, an idea, *all because he was a tither.*

Would God do such things today? Without a doubt, YES. How does God give us good spoken words? Through dreams, words of knowledge, words of wisdom, etc., *but generally, guidance comes through our spirits.* Proverbs 20:27 tells us the spirit of man is the candle of the Lord.

The spirit of man is the candle of the Lord...
                - Proberbs 20:27

In other words, *our spirits is where God is going to give us direction and guidance.* Another way to say this is, our spirits is where God shines His light to show us the path that we need to follow. And when God's people become tithers and givers, God gives us *financial* guidance *in our spirits.* He drops good spoken words into our

153

spirits creating ideas to make money.

What we see with Jacob is that here was a man who had never become a financial success. This is not to say that he had never tried to be a financial success. His whole life was a life of wheeling and dealing trying to get ahead, yet time and time again he ended back where he started. But when God spoke and revealed a plan for success, his life began to take a turn for the better. Although God's plan took some time before it all came to pass, the turn started when Jacob received his good spoken word, his God-inspired idea.

If you, too, have tried over and over to succeed, and yet success has always seemed to have eluded you, make the decision to become a tither and a giver of offerings. Tithes and offerings open the windows of heaven to allow God to drop good spoken words into our spirits. These creative ideas will take you to higher levels of success. Although your ultimate goal is to get from A to Z, if for years you've never been able to leave point A, point B sure will look and feel good. As you are faithful, points C,D,E,F, etc. will also surely come to pass. Success with God is a progression. The scripture plainly states we grow from glory to glory and faith to yet greater faith.

THE WIDOW WOMAN

Now there cried a certain woman of the wives of the sons of the prophets unto Elisha, saying, Thy servant my husband is dead...and the creditor is come to take unto him my two sons to be bondmen.

- II Kings 4:1

154

This widow woman received an unusual good spoken word to help her out of a tough situation. She had been married to one of the sons of the prophets that Elisha had been a teacher over. You'll notice in verse 1 she said, "*Thy* servant *my* husband is dead." Sad to say, after her husband's death she was so far in debt the creditor had made the decision to make her two sons slaves. Needless to say, she was more than a little upset. She then came to Elisha for help, and take note of what Elisha asked her:

…what hast thou in the house?

She replied,

…Thine handmaid hath not any thing in the house, save a pot of oil.

Evidently, any possessions she may have possessed had been taken from her to repay a portion of her debt. All that was left was *one* pot of oil. Up to this point, things had not been good for this woman. But this is where the story changes. She received a good spoken word from God through the man of God, Elisha.

Elisha instructed her to borrow as many pots as she could get hold of and bring them into her house:

Then he (Elisha) said, Go, borrow thee vessels abroad of all thy neighbors, even empty vessels; BORROW NOT A FEW.

So she obeyed what Elisha told her to do, and went to ALL of her neighbors and borrowed many, many, many pots. Once she got them into her house she shut the door behind her, grabbed the one pot of oil she had and, according to Elisha's instruction, started pouring oil into all of the empty borrowed pots. The amazing miracle was, *her one pot of oil never ran out of oil!* She kept pouring and the oil kept flowing. In fact, according to verse 6, the oil didn't stop flowing until ALL of the empty pots were filled.

This leads into another interesting point -- *The size of this woman's miracle was dependent upon how many pots she borrowed*. If she would've only borrowed a few pots she would have limited the size of the miracle God was wanting to perform. This shows that we play an integral part in the size of our miracles. God has the ability to work any size miracle, yet He works in conjunction with the size of our faith. Elisha was very plain about it. He said in verse 3, "borrow NOT A FEW."

In other words, if she would've only borrowed 35 pots she would've only gotten 35 pots of oil. If she would've borrowed 75 pots she would've gotten 75 pots of oil. If she would've borrowed 150 pots she would've gotten 150 pots of oil, etc. Again, the size of her miracle was based upon the number of pots she brought into her house. *Evidently, the size of the miracle we receive from God is dependent upon how much we allow God to bless us*.

Once all of the pots were miraculously filled Elisha gave her further direction:

...And he said, Go, sell the oil, AND PAY THY DEBT, and live thou and thy children of the rest.
- II Kings 4:7

Because of this *good spoken word* from God, **she was miraculously freed from ALL her debt**. But not only was her debt paid off, she also had enough money *left over* for her and her family to live on:

156

TITHES AND OFFERINGS BRING MONEY-MAKING IDEAS

...Go, sell the oil, and pay thy debt, AND LIVE THOU AND THY CHILDREN OF THE REST.

- II Kings 4:7

You see, God has a way to get you out of debt AND a way to get you into abundance. The key is to hear what God is speaking to us. *Also, notice that this woman still had to work.* God gave her the creative idea, but it was up to her to put action to that idea. *First*, she had to gather many, many pots. She had to go from neighbor to neighbor inquiring about unused pots. *Secondly*, she then had to carry the pots back to her house. I seriously doubt she had a mule or donkey to load the pots on to take home. All of her possessions had been taken from her. They were even ready to take her two sons as well. So, she had to bundle up the pots in sacks, or whatever, and lug those pots home, over and over, again and again. *Thirdly,* she then had to fill the empty pots with oil. Since her one pot of oil never became empty she was having to lug a full pot all over her house, and then having to lift that full pot up to pour into all of the other pots, over and over. I'm sure by the time she was through she was weary from all the exhausting work. And *fourthly*, she then had to sell the oil. Selling is not necessarily the easiest thing to do. But that's what she had to do.

The lesson here is, when God drops a good spoken word into our spirit, we're still going to have to put legs to that idea. Some people just do not want to work. They want the prosperity but not the work. They want the wealth, but they don't want to have to "get" that wealth. But realize this, God doesn't bless laziness. God has much to say in the Bible about the sluggard and sloth-fulness. They'll end up or remain in poverty.

Financial prosperity is the result of 1) a God-inspired idea, and 2) obeying God's idea *with work*. If we're willing to work, God will bless whatever it is we put our hand to do (Deut. 28:8, Joshua 1:8). Realize this also, no matter how far in debt you may be, God has a way to get you out and to keep you out. From the worldly, economic standpoint it may look financially impossible, but I remind you, what is impossible with man is possible with God. God has the necessary idea to get you from where you are to where you want to be.

This leads into another thought -- Should the poor be instructed to tithe and give offerings? Most definitely yes.

YES, THE POOR SHOULD TITHE AND GIVE OFFERINGS

Since God drops good spoken words into the spirits of those who tithe and give offerings, and since these good spoken words result in financial prosperity, the poor should most definitely be encouraged to tithe and give offerings. To instruct the poor not to tithe and not to give offerings is to keep the windows of heaven closed to them and to keep them bound and imprisoned in poverty.

If there's one group of people that needs financially creative ideas *it's the poor.* Their higher educational possibilities are limited, their job prospects are limited, and a poverty mentality has been ingrained into their thinking. So something is going to have to change. They *need* good spoken words dropped into their spirits. And tithes and offerings is the key.

CHAPTER
16

TITHES AND OFFERINGS BRING MONEY-MAKING IDEAS FROM GOD - PART 2

...I will open you the windows of heaven, and pour you out a BLESSING, that there shall not be room enough to receive it.

- Malachi 3:10

As we brought out in the preceding chapter, this word "blessing" can also be translated "benediction." This word "benediction" is composed of two parts, 1) bene, and 2) diction. "Bene" means "good," and "diction" means "spoken word." Thus, Bene-diction means "good spoken word."

...I will open you the windows of heaven, and pour you out a GOOD SPOKEN WORD...

- Malachi 3:10 (author's privilege)

This good spoken word results in a financial blessing that's so large we won't have room enough to contain it all. A good spoken word means "creative ideas."

...I will open you the windows of heaven, and pour you out a CREATIVE IDEA...

- Malachi 3:10 (author's privilege)

You see, God gives us the power to _get_ wealth. God gives us the _idea_, and _we_ bring the wealth in. Also notice, the word "windows" is in its plural form:

...I will open you the WINDOW_S_ of heaven...
- Malachi 3:10

This means that God doesn't just drop _one_ good spoken word, or idea, into our spirit. This means that God drops _many_ good spoken words, _many_ creative ideas into our spirit. Each idea can be a means of blessing us financially as we progress in our financial growth.

Because we haven't been taught _how_ God prospers us I think many of us have missed many, many creative ideas God has dropped into our spirits. Fortunately, God is ever continuing to drop good spoken words into our spirits. As we become more "spirit-conscious" we'll be better able to pick up on what God is speaking to our spirits. Let's look at two more scriptural examples of how God has blessed others.

PETER

...Launch out into the deep, and let down your nets for a draught.
- Jesus to Peter, Luke 5:4

Peter received a good spoken word that caused an immediate abundance in his life. Peter had been a professional fisherman, along with his brother Andrew. According to verse 10 they had formed a partnership with James and John, who you'll remember from Mark 1:20 had even hired people to work for them. Obviously they had possessed a successful fishing business.

Now to the point -- Peter had _given_ the use of his boat to Jesus for the ministry of the Word. After Jesus had ministered to the people he turned to Peter and instructed him to launch back out into the deep and let down his nets for a draught. _This was Peter's good spoken word._ **_Giving always precedes good spoken words._**

Previously, Peter had spent the whole night without any success:

And Simon answering said unto him, Master, we have toiled all the night, and have taken nothing...
- Luke 5:5

But past failure has nothing to do with preventing future success _if we act on what God says._ This is a critical lesson to learn. When God gives us a good spoken word we must learn to forget about any defeats or failures we experienced in the past. Tithers and givers have God's promise that the devourer will be rebuked. Success is now ours for the taking. Peter refused to allow the previous night's failure to dictate his obeying what Jesus said to do.

And Simon answering said unto him, Master, we have toiled all the night, and have taken nothing: *NEVERTHELESS* AT THY WORD I WILL LET DOWN THE NET. **- Luke 5:5**

Peter acted on his good spoken word. He went out to the deep and lowered his net. _The result was a great multitude of fishes._

Several lessons here -- 1) Peter's good spoken word came _after_ Peter had given his boat to Jesus to use. Giving always precedes receiving. Good spoken words come
161

to people who give.

2) This idea Jesus gave to Peter was not necessarily an unusual idea. After all, fishermen fish most of the time. That's their job. The point is, the idea God gives _you_, in all probability, won't be something completely alien or foreign to what you're familiar with.

The mistake some have made is to think that they're going to have to reinvent the wheel all over again -- a new kind of ballbearing, or discover a new form of power like electricity. And though God does give some of His people these kinds of _inventive_ ideas, it doesn't necessarily mean God will do this for you. What's important is that God gives you a _creative_ idea, _a good spoken word._ What Peter did (lowering the net) was something he did all the time. _The difference was that this time Peter lowered the net in obedience to God's instruction._ The result was a great multitude of fish which, to a fisherman, is prosperity.

3) It's important to follow our good spoken word _precisely,_ or to ask questions until we _understand_ precisely. For example, Jesus told Peter to launch back into the deep, and let down his _nets_ (v.4). Notice that Jesus didn't say _net_, singular, but instead _nets_, plural. But what did Peter do? He said, "I will let down the _net_," singular (v.5). Verse 6 then records, "...and their _net_ (singular) brake."

Peter still received his great miracle, but he wound up with a torn net. Had his partners already been out there with him Peter's net would have still been in one piece. The point is, when God drops a good spoken word into our spirit, **it's up to us** to seek God until we **fully** understand so that we can better comply for a greater miracle.

4) The size of our miracle is determined by how many nets we lower. In the preceding chapter we saw that the widow woman's miracle was dependent upon how many pots she gathered. Here we again see the correlation between how much we plan for, and the size of the miracle we receive. To every miracle there is a God-ward part and a man-ward part. God does His part and man has to do his part.

Here in Luke 5 God had the "miracle fish" in place swimming below the boat, **but how many fish that were caught was dependant upon how many nets were lowered by Peter.** The size of our miracle much of the time is more dependant upon _us_ than upon God. God has already put the miracle in motion, but now it's up to us to bring in how many fish we made preparation for. The lesson is, we need to think much bigger and believe much bigger than we have in the past. The miracles we've received in the past could have been much bigger if we would have made greater preparation for them. And the miracles awaiting us in the future can be much larger if we'll make the decision to begin preparing now. Think big, plan big, and believe big.

WATER INTO WINE

And when they wanted wine, the mother of Jesus saith unto him, They have no wine.
- John 2:3

I find it extremely interesting that the very first miracle Jesus performed in his earthly ministry was a miracle of luxury. Turning water into wine for a marriage feast was certainly not a need. Everyone had already had their fill of wine. Their need, if even this can be called a need, had already been supplied earlier in the feast. Yet when Jesus worked this miracle of producing _additional_ wine, the wine He ended up supplying was _superior_ to any that had already been served (John 2:10). Without a doubt, this "additional" and "superior" wine was an _extra_, a miracle of luxury, not a need.

Again we see that God is not only interested in meeting our needs, He's interested in granting us our desires and wants. God wants you to have what you _want_. When Jesus multiplied the loaves and fishes to feed the 5,000, the scripture states the multitude was able to partake of the food until they had _as much as they would_ (John 6:11). You see, God wants us to have just as much as we want. _Our_ desires, what _we_ want, means a whole lot to God.

Now to our point -- what caused this miracle of luxury to begin? _A good spoken word_! Notice:

...WHATSOEVER HE SAITH UNTO YOU, do it.

- John 2:5

This is how financial increase comes about -- _doing what God tells us to do._ As we've already brought out, this is what Malachi 3:10 calls, "good spoken words." God reveals to our spirits "ideas" for prosperity. **And as we act on what God shows us to do,** our water, so to speak, will turn into wine. In other words, our _ordinary_ finances will turn into _superior_ finances. Just as the miracle wine was superior in value to the ordinary water, so will our "good spoken word finances" be superior in value to our "ordinary" finances. But this increase in value in our finances comes in obedience to doing what God tells us to do. John 2:5 is as clear as it gets. **This miracle was the result of a good spoken word from Jesus.**

Also, what Jesus told them to do required some effort on their part. Jesus told them to fill the waterpots with water (John 2:7). According to verse 6, there were 6 waterpots of stone, with each pot containing 2 or 3 firkins. A firkin was 9 gallons. Thus, each waterpot contained a minimum of 18 gallons and as much as 27 gallons. Since there were 6 waterpots of stone, they had to draw from the well between 108 gallons to 162 gallons of water to carry back to the feast. Assuming the well bucket was a gallon bucket, they had to draw between 108 to 162 times. And as anyone who has drawn from a well will tell you, that is a lot of hard work. Then once it was drawn, the heavy water had to be carried back to where the feast was being celebrated.

The point is (again), the good spoken word God drops into our spirits will require some effort on our part. God will give us the idea, but it's up to us to work out the planning, the details, the production, the evaluating, the loose ends, and the sometimes difficult labor. It may not be easy, but the reward will be worth it many times over. If we're willing to work it, assuming we're tithers and givers, God will drop good spoken words into our spirits that will produce financial blessings.

Incidentally, Jacob's son, Joseph, enjoyed a miracle of luxury because of a good spoken word. His good spoken word came in the form of an understanding of a dream. And when his miracle came to pass he wasn't just let out of prison, *which most people would have been content with,* but God promoted him to 2nd in command over all of Egypt. *God has a way to get you out of a prison of debt and into exceeding abundance.*

When life may look its worst, and when failure appears to have become a lifestyle, *success is only one good spo-*

ken word away. God revealed to Joseph a 7-year bumper crop and a 7 year famine that Egypt was getting ready to go through. In effect, God gave Joseph a savings plan for the good years that would help them ride out the bad years. *The end result is that in just one day Joseph left the prison and became the 2nd richest man in all of Egypt.*

SUMMARY

The whole Bible is full of provisionary miracles because of good spoken words God gave to his servants. When the children of Israel needed water to drink, God gave **Moses** a good spoken word. He told Moses to speak to a rock. The result was a miracle of water. **Isaac** prospered because of a good spoken word during a famine (Gen. 26:1-3, 12-13). **Elijah** was taken care of during a famine because of a good spoken word (1 Kings 17:3-4, 17:9). The **widow of Zarephath** enjoyed provision during a famine because of a good spoken word (1 Kings 17: 8-16). **Peter** received his tribute money because of a good spoken word from Jesus (Matt. 17:27) The list goes on and on.

Just exactly *how* God will prosper you is unknown. Don't do what God told someone else to do just because they experienced success from it. The reason they succeeded was because they did what God told *them* to do. *Your* success will come because you do what God tells *you* to do.

For example, God may give some people the ability to prosper by investing in the Stock Market. Others may get the word to invest in commodities. God may give some a creative idea for something completely new on the market. Yet God may give others the ability to market an already existing idea. And yet others may prosper by a real estate investment. (You could be led to an unknown piece of property that, in 5 years, could be worth 10 times as much as it is now.)

For example, I met one man who "felt" impressed to buy a certain piece of property. He was a member of a good church, and supported his church with his tithes and supported various traveling ministers with his offerings. He told me that God led him to purchase a certain piece of property. 8 months later that certain piece of property became "prime" real estate. To make a long story short, he was offered a sum of money that allowed him to profit $813,000 on that one deal. He experienced financial increase because of a good spoken word.

So it's important to allow God to speak to us. *But don't get involved in real estate just because it worked for someone else.* It may not work the same for you. The above man prospered because God told *him* to do it. He didn't get involved in computer chips, DAT recorders, or hard disk television equipment. Why? Because God didn't lead him that way. God led *him* to a piece of property. He succeeded because he didn't pay any attention to computer chips, DAT recorders, or hard disk television equipment. You will succeed only if you do what God tells **you** to do.

God's next step for you might be a promotion at your present job, with better pay and better benefits. And yet God might lead you to a completely different job. But don't leave your present job until you have the better job wrapped up. It's amazing what some people do under the assumption of God supposedly speaking. **Don't rush into the unknown.** Isaiah 28:16 says, "*...they that believe shall not make haste.*" So take your time. Weigh things out in your mind and in your spirit. If there's a small hesitancy, wait it out. Maybe the timing isn't right. Maybe certain things need to fall into place before you can do what you're supposed to do. Maybe, though, what you're thinking about is not even an idea from God.

Time is not against you. If someone tries to pressure you into making a quick decision, back away from it. Too many mistakes have been made by people who rushed a decision. Don't ever allow anyone to force you into anything. Even if the idea was from God, *but if you felt rushed*, God will give you **another** good spoken word. Remember, Malachi 3:10 tells us that God will open the *windows* of heaven. God has more than one idea up his sleeve for you. *Don't ever make a hasty decision.*

God realizes that we're living in a fallen world. God knows there are many voices in the world clamoring for our attention, some good but many bad. We need to be careful. If we miss an opportunity trying to do what's right, God is not limited that He can't bless us with other ideas. One time I heard a preacher say that it's better to be too slow than too fast. If we're too fast we'll jump out ahead of God and make a mess of things on our own. If we're slow we can at least see God out in front of us and follow His lead.

What's most important is that we tithe and give offerings. Tithes and offerings bring money-making ideas from God. As we're faithful in seeking first the kingdom of God and his righteousness, God will continue to drop good spoken words into our spirits. As we develop in our ability to listen to our spirits, we'll hear what God is saying to us more and more.

CHAPTER
17

THE SIZE OF OUR OFFERING DETERMINES THE AMOUNT OF MONEY OUR GOD-GIVEN IDEA WILL PRODUCE

Give, and it shall be given unto you; good measure, pressed down, and shaken together, and running over, shall men give into your bosom. FOR WITH THE SAME MEASURE THAT YE METE WITHAL IT SHALL BE MEASURED TO YOU AGAIN.

- Luke 6:38

As we've established in the previous two chapters, God gives good spoken words, also called creative ideas, to people who are tithers and givers. These ideas, if acted upon, will cause a financial increase in our lives. But it's important to point out, just *how much* of a financial increase that comes to us is first determined by *how much we've previously sown.* A harvest is always in direct proportion to how much seed is planted. As the apostle Paul pointed out in II Corinthians 9:6, if we sow sparingly we will reap also sparingly, but if we sow bountifully we will reap also bountifully. Thus, *how much we give determines how much is given to us.*

Of course, if we give this doesn't mean that outright strangers will walk up to us on the street and give us money, although it's technically possible that this could happen. This is a misunderstood interpretation of Jesus' words in Luke 6:38, "*...shall men give into your bosom.*" This just simply means that how money comes to us will be *through men*, through this worldly money system. The help will come from heaven, but not the money. The money will come through the hands of men in the world through buying, selling, trading, bank interest, etc. Generally, what happens is that God gives us ideas, that if implemented in the world, cause financial increase to come to us.

With this in mind, take note of the following two scriptures again:

...For with the same measure that ye mete withal it shall be measured to you again.
- Jesus, Luke 6:38

But this I say, He which soweth sparingly shall reap also sparingly; and he which soweth bountifully shall reap also bountifully.
- Paul, II Corinthians 9:6

As you can see, Jesus and Paul are saying the same thing. How much we give determines how much we get. And since money comes through the good spoken words God drops into our spirits, this means the ideas God gives to us are in direct relation to how much we sow. If we sow a little God will give us an idea that will produce a little. If we sow much God will give us an idea that will produce much more.

This is why it's not good to try to copy what God has told someone else to do. The reason they're a success at what they're doing is because God told them to do it. The reason they're prospering in it to such a high financial degree is because they've planted much in the kingdom of God. They're just simply reaping what they've been sowing.

But if you haven't planted as much into the kingdom of God as they have, and if you try to copy what they're doing, you could end up making a mess of things for yourself, *because you're trying to reap a harvest much larger than the degree to which you've sown.*

It's extremely important to stay within the confines of what God speaks to your spirit. God will give you an idea that will produce a harvest in direct proportion to the size of what you've planted. As you're faithful in your giving, and as you're able to increase your giving, God will give you a new idea. Maybe it will be further insight into the idea He's already given you that will produce a much greater harvest. Or maybe God will tell you to forget the previous idea because it's gone as far as it can go. And He'll give you a completely different idea with a much greater profit potential.

How much we prosper is not up to God, it's up to us. We can either reap sparingly or bountifully, *depending upon how much we plant.* Secondly, it's important to learn how to follow God's leading in our spirit. *Our success or failure to prosper could hinge on this.* Since, generally speaking, these good spoken words come to us in our spirits, it's necessary to learn how to recognize when God is dealing with us. This is not to say that God won't give us a dream or something a little more spectacular, but the scriptures are emphatic that it's through our

171

spirits that God deals with His children 99% of the time.

For as many as are led BY THE SPIRIT of God, they are the sons of God.
- Romans 8:14

The SPIRIT itself (Himself) beareth witness WITH OUR SPIRIT, that we are the children of God.
- Romans 8:16

God leads us *in our spirits* by the Spirit of God. God bears witness with our spirit concerning everything with which our lives have to do -- from salvation to divine protection to financial leadings. When the apostle Paul was being transported by ship to Rome he tried to dissuade the captain from sailing. Why? Because he had an *unrest in his spirit.* He *perceived* that something wasn't right.

Now when much time was spent, and when sailing was now dangerous, because the fast was now already past, Paul admonished them, And said unto them, Sirs, *I PERCEIVE* that this voyage will be with hurt and much damage, not only of the lading and ship, but also of our lives.
- Acts 27:9,10

Notice that Paul didn't say he had a vision, or that he had heard the audible voice of God. *He simply had an inward perception.* He *perceived* that things were not as they should be.

It's this kind of a leading that God will use to lead us in our finances -- an inward perception, or as the scripture also calls it, the Holy Spirit bearing witness with our spirits. We'll either have an inside-velvety-good feeling or an inside-bad-"yucky" feeling. As we learn to follow our spirits, God will be able to bless us more and more.

So don't do things just because other people seem to be having success from them. *You* do what God leads *you* to do. And as *you* are faithful in doing what *you* are supposed to do success will come to *you*.

Maybe someone will come to you with something that appears it'll easily make a hundred million dollars. But if there's an unrest on the inside of you, don't make a move. God could be leading you to not get involved. Maybe there are things there that haven't been brought to your attention. Or maybe it's a scam. Or maybe it's going to bomb. Who knows? Who cares, if God is leading you away from it. Don't do things or get involved with things if there's the *slightest* check on the inside of you. Even if there's just the smallest, teeny-weeny *if*, don't budge an inch. If you'll learn to follow God's leadings, He'll protect you, guide you, and lead you. As we're faithful in our tithes and offerings, God's purpose is to take us from harvest to bigger harvest to greater harvest, etc.

GIVE AS YOU ARE ABLE

For who hath despised the day of small things?
- Zechariah 4:10

For God, who gives seed to the farmer to plant, and later on, good crops to harvest to eat, will give you MORE AND MORE SEED TO PLANT and make it grow so that you can give away more and more fruit from your harvest.
- II Corinthians 9:10, *The Living Bible*

Some people reading this book may be so far in debt it may look as if there's no way out. Every dollar is already

173

accounted for. The creditors know when your payday is, and they're ready to collect every paycheck down to the dime. Or maybe your medical expenses are through the roof. It looks as if you'll be trying to pay off the hospital for the next 40 years. And the question that has come to me is, "*Where can I get some money to sow? I don't have anything and there's not any way I can get anything. Is there any hope for me?*"

Yes, there's hope for you. This may surprise you, but you do have something to give. Maybe you have an extra cake mix in the cabinet. If so, bake a cake and give it to your pastor. If you have some left over change in your pocket, maybe 2 dimes, a nickel, and 4 pennies, put it in an envelope and give it to your church. Even if you only have an extra pair of shoestrings, you have something to give. Don't ridicule or despise these small beginnings. I remind you of Zechariah 4:10. *Don't despise the day of small things!* What's important at this point is that you get started. As you make the decision to be a giver, you'll be amazed at what you'll find around the house that you can give.

Most importantly, God sees your *heart* to be a giver. God sees where you're at, He knows what you've been through, and He's got a specially designed plan just for you to get you from where you are to where you need to be. So don't get upset with your small beginnings. Your harvests may not appear to be much, but the fact is, God's getting you to a systematic plan of sowing and reaping.

The beginning of your harvests may seem to be nothing more than a couple of extra hours of overtime at work. But it's starting to happen. Eventually you might get a raise, or a better work-benefit program. But one thing you'll start to notice, your money that seemed to be put into pockets with holes (Haggai 1:6) will start staying in your pockets. The turn-around has begun. Ideas, opportunities, favor, getting breaks, etc., will start coming your way. As you're faithful with the little, God will continue to bring more and more your way. There's even a scripture that talks about witty inventions:

I wisdom dwell with prudence, and find out knowledge of witty inventions.
- Proverbs 8:12

Anything is possible with God. Sowing and reaping is miraculous. II Corinthians 9:6-11 and Malachi 3: 8-12 is just as true as John 3:16. When we begin we may only be able to give a little, but as time goes on, we'll be able to give more and more. Correspondingly, the harvests will at first be small, but in time the harvests will grow.

For example, if you can only give 2 nickels, your harvest will be in direct proportion to your giving of the 2 nickels. From that harvest you might be able to give 3 nickels. As a result, your next harvest will be in direct proportion to your giving of the 3 nickels. From that harvest you might be able to give a dollar. Thus, your new harvest will be in direct proportion to your giving of the dollar. From that new harvest you might be able to give 10 dollars. Again, your next harvest will be in direct proportion to your giving of the 10 dollars. From this harvest you might be able to give 20 dollars. Your next harvest will now be in direct proportion to the giving of the 20 dollars. From that harvest you might be able to give 30 dollars. Look at II Corinthians 9:10 again:

PIECING TOGETHER THE PROSPERITY PUZZLE

For God, who gives seed to the farmer to plant, and later on, good crops to harvest to eat, will give you MORE AND MORE SEED TO PLANT and make it grow SO THAT YOU CAN GIVE AWAY MORE AND MORE FRUIT FROM YOUR HARVEST.
- II Corinthians 9:10, *The Living Bible*

When we plant we get a harvest. From the harvest we have *more* seed to plant. When we plant more seed we get a larger harvest. From the larger harvest we have even more seed to plant. When we plant even more seed we get an even larger harvest. This is God's plan to get you out of debt and into abundance.

From this we can see that 10 million dollar ideas don't come from 10 cent offerings. But as we're faithful in the 10 cent offerings we'll be able to move into 25 cent offerings. From the 25 cent offerings we'll be able to move into the dollar offerings. From the dollar offerings we'll be able to move into the 10 dollar offerings. And as our harvests grow so will our offerings grow. As our offerings grow so will our harvests grow again. It's an ongoing cycle that starts small but has no limit. We're only limited by how small we think and believe.

Ideas, bigger ideas, and even greater ideas will eventually come. Don't get upset because you haven't been given a "big" idea yet. Don't look at a small idea as not being worthy of your attention. *It's one step among many steps.* Many times bigger ideas require bigger capital, so even if God did give you a "big" idea you wouldn't be in a financial position to do anything about it. So God is going to start you where you're able. The key is to get started. We may have to stay faithful at a particular level for awhile, but sooner or later increase will come. Steadily we'll find ourselves climbing out of the hole we dug ourselves into. Good spoken words will come.

CHAPTER
18

HOW TO GIVE

6 But this I say, He which soweth sparingly shall reap also sparingly; and he which soweth bountifully shall reap also bountifully.

7 Every man according as he purposeth in his heart, so let him give; not grudgingly, or of necessity: for God loveth a cheerful giver.

8 And God is able to make all grace abound toward you: that ye, always having all suffiencey in all things may abound to every good work:

9 (As it is written, He hath dispersed abroad; he hath given to the poor; his righteousness remaineth forever.

10 Now he that ministereth seed to the sower both minister bread for your food, and multiply your seed sown, and increase the fruits of your righteousness;)

11 Being enriched in everything to all bountifulness, which causeth through us thanksgiving to God.

- II Corinthians 9:6-11

This is an extremely exciting subject. Our giving causes a supernatual connection that allows God to work in our finances in a miraculous way. To not give is a serious mistake that hinders God from doing in our finances what He really wants to do. God loves a cheerful giver, and to the person who chooses a lifestyle of giving, God involves Himself in their finances. And the most amazing and remarkable things can and will happen.

To begin, II Corinthians 9:6-11 is not talking about tithing. Here's why -- 1) Verse 9 says, "He hath dispersed *abroad*...". The tithe is not dispersed abroad, the tithe goes to the storehouse. 2) Verse 9 also says, "he hath given to the *poor*...". The tithe does not go to the poor. Again, the tithe goes to the storehouse. 3) Verse 6 tells us we can give *sparingly or bountifully*. The tithe is not a discretionary amount, the tithe is always a set 10 percent. Clearly, II Corinthians 9:6-11 is teaching about offerings.

Offerings are an intergral part of the Christian walk. Our giving allows God to give to us. There are three principals to know concerning offerings -- 1) how to give, 2) the seed must die, and 3) the size of the offering determines the size of the harvest. Let's look at these.

1. How to give.

Every man as he purposeth in his heart, so let him give; NOT GRUDGINGLY, or OF NECESSITY: for God loveth a CHEERFUL GIVER.
- II Corinthians 9:7

As far as God is concerned, it's not the money that is given, it's HOW the money is given. God doesn't take pleasure in offerings that are given sorrowfully or unwillingly by people who feel forced to give. God takes pleasure in people who give *because they want to give*. God looks at the heart. Notice:

And Jesus sat over against the treasury, and beheld HOW the people cast money into the treasury...
- Mark 12:41

It's important to point out that just as Jesus took note of *how* people gave 2,000 years ago, He takes note of

178

how people give today. God takes note of the people who give from a willing heart and the people who give from an unwilling heart. God blesses *cheerful* givers, not *sorrowful* givers. If we want to enjoy financial prosperity, our heart is going to have to take pleasure in giving.

A LIFESTYLE OF GIVING

Notice that this scripture doesn't say God loves a cheerful GIFT, He loves a cheerful GIVER. This is talking about a **lifestyle** of giving, **LIVING to give**. The abundant prosperity II Corinthians 9:6-11 is telling us about is available for the person whose *heart* is one of giving.

Sad to say, some people hear Bible teaching on prosperity, and because they want prosperity, they give, not because of a love and appreciation for God and His work, but because of greed. And because their motive is wrong, God can't bless their giving. God wants to bless them financially, but God can't because of the condition of their heart. God is looking for a *giver*, not a *gift.*

A *giver* is a person whose whole lifestyle is one of giving. It's not just when people pull their checkbooks out at church for tithes or offerings that makes them givers. How do they give when they're not at church? A *giver* will be giving all day, all week, all month, and all year.

For example, how do you drive in town or on the freeway? Do you allow people to squeeze in front of you when they need to take the next exit, or do you drive in such a way that they have no choice but to find a space somewhere behind you? As silly as this may sound, it's everyday incidents like these that reveal what's in our hearts. What about people in the grocery store? Do you ever allow people with fewer items than you to freely cut in front of you at the checkout line, or do you always make them get behind? Are you always one to take home from work things like paper clips, pens, erasers, etc. because you feel it's owed to you? Are you one who always expects backrubs from your spouse, but never one who gives any? What about your neighbors? Do you mow the lawn only to the property edge because you don't want to end up mowing more than you have to?

The point is, some people live their whole lives with an attitude of take, take, take. They feel that life always owes them a break, and they're out to "get" what they can. When they hear about Biblical prosperity, they carry with them this same attitude. They may give offerings, but they don't do it with a pure heart. And when prosperity never seems to come their way, they get mad, throw up their hands, and argue about why Biblical prosperity doesn't work.

It's important to think about developing our heart. Our heart may need to be cultivated. We may need to "practice" awhile. Some people can make a heart change right away, others need time to weed out the old and bring in the new. For some, it may take some time to oust the "take, take, take" attitude and develop a lifestyle of "give, give, give." **But once it's cultivated the blessings will follow right behind.** God doesn't look on the outside, God looks on the heart.

2. The seed must die.

...so let him give...

- II Corinthians 9:7

To give is *to release*. It means *to relinquish possession of, to let loose of*. When we *give* an offering we turn loose *without any strings attached.* It no longer belongs to us. Unless we specify when we give it where we want it to go (building project, missionary project, etc.), we relinquish control of it. It then belongs to that minister, ministry, or church to use in the way they see fit.

Sad to say, some people give offerings with ulterior motives. They give with a motive to control the minister or church they give to. In effect, they're trying to "buy" that minister. Some people have an agenda that they want implemented in a church or ministry, and they think if they give an offering it should give them a say-so in what should be done. They want to influence that minister to do what they want done. Their purpose in giving is not that *God's* work will get done, but that *their* work will get done.

Offerings are very sacred to God. And to abuse an offering for personal ambition is not only wrong, in many cases it's evil. Some people give offerings with the hopes it will influence the minister to put them on the church board, or to put them in some kind of a leadership position in the church. But this is not right. If we give offerings with intents such as these we'll never reap anything good, certainly nothing with God's blessing.

When we give an offering we give with no strings attached. We're not looking to man, or to the person we give to to give us results. We want *God* to produce a harvest.

OFFERINGS MUST BE PLANTED IN APPROPRIATE SOIL

Some people want to use tithes and offerings as money they give to themselves, or to their children, or for their houses. I know one couple who used to tithe to their

181

PIECING TOGETHER THE PROSPERITY PUZZLE

church and give offerings to traveling ministers, but they made the decision to use their money normally desig-nated for tithes and offerings to build their own dream house. They tried to justify this in their mind by saying that if any traveling minister needed to spend the night or get away for awhile, they would have a "prophet's cham-ber" (actually, a spare room) that this minister could sleep in. But this is unscriptural. The tithe goes to the store-house, not _your_ house (Mal. 3:10), and offerings go "to him (the minister) that teacheth" (Gal. 6:6).

Other people want to use their tithes and offerings as money they use to help their children. Sometimes when children grow up and get started on their own they face some difficult financial times. And we certainly do want to help our children. In fact, it's scripturally correct to do so (1 Tim. 5:8). But some people want to use their tithe and offering money for this. And this is where they're missing it. Though their children could certainly use it, and no doubt would appreciate it, a financial harvest doesn't grow from this.

Other people want to use their tithes and offerings for their children's education. And as is well noted, a college education is extremely expensive. Our children need all the help they can get. The problem, though, with some well-meaning people is that they want to dip into their tithes and offerings for this and call paying for a college education an _offering_. Clearly, this is not an offering.

God has a way to bless us so that we can have a nice house, help our children, and pay for a college education. That's what this whole book is all about. God has a way to prosper His people, **and tithes and offerings is the key.** But tithes and offerings have to be planted _in the appro-priate ground._ When planted correctly, God can oversee a financial harvest that will allow for abundance to help our children, etc. Here's what has to take place -- *the seed (offering money) has to first "die."* Let me explain.

A SEED HAS TO DIE

Verily, verily I say unto you, except a corn of wheat fall into the ground AND DIE, it abideth alone: but if it die, IT BRINGETH FORTH MUCH FRUIT.

- Jesus, John 12:24

To produce a crop, a seed, as Jesus explained, had to die. For our understanding, *it means it had to enter a period of uselessness to the planter.* Before a seed is planted, a farmer can do with it what he wants -- sell it, eat it, or let the livestock feed on it. But once he *plants* a seed, that seed can no longer be used by the farmer for other purposes. That planted seed enters a time period when he can't do anything with it. Why? It's gone. It's dead. But by it dying, at a later time, it will become of much more use than it ever could have as a seed.

And this is how our offerings, our financial seeds, must become to us. We relinquish possession of them, we let loose of them, all attached strings are cut. *The use of that money dies to us.* We can no longer benefit from it, we GIVE it. We're not looking to the person we give it to for results, *we're looking to God for results.* God is the source for our harvest, not man. We're not "buying" something from man, we're *giving* it to God. We may be "planting" it in a man's ministry, but we're giving it to God.

183

3. The size of the offering determines the size of the harvest.

The apostle Paul refers to offerings as "seeds." He calls giving "sowing." And he calls financial increase "reaping."

But this I say, He which soweth sparingly shall reap also sparingly: and he which soweth bountifully shall reap also bountifully.

- II Corinthians 9:6

Notice how *THE LIVING BIBLE* paraphrases this verse:

But remember this -- if you give little, you will get little. A farmer who plants just a few seeds will get only a small crop, but if he plants much, he will reap much.

- II Corinthians 9:6, *THE LIVING BIBLE*

You see, if we give little, using farmer terminology, it means we are sowing little. And as any farmer will tell you, the one who only sows a little won't have much of a harvest. To be a successful farmer, one has to sow *much,* a whole lot, **because the size of the harvest is in direct proportion to the size of the sowing.** Likewise, to enjoy financial increase we have to sow much, i.e. we have to *give* much.

Giving produces increase. Hoarding results in decrease. To plant one acre of seed produces one acre of harvest. *But to plant 1,000 acres of seed produces 1,000 acres of harvest.* Suprising to most Christians, how much we prosper is not up to God, *it's up to us.* As Paul said, we can reap sparingly or we can reap bountifully, depending on how much we sow.

184

This fits in beautifully with what Jesus said in Luke 6:38:

Give, and it shall be given unto you; good measure, pressed down, and shaken together, and running over, shall men give into your bosom. FOR WITH THE SAME MEASURE THAT YE METE IT SHALL BE MEASURED TO YOU AGAIN.
- Luke 6:38

As you can see, this is not referring to the tithe. The tithe is always a set 10 percent. This is echoing what Paul said in II Corinthians 9:6, or actually, I should say that Paul is echoing what Jesus said. *Jesus has made it clear that the size of how much we give determines the size of how much we receive.* It cannot be given unto us until we first give. But just *how much* is given to us is based on *how much* is first given in the offering.

It's important to realize that God *wants* us all to have incredibly huge harvests. God wants us to reap so much that we don't have room enough to contain it all. Why? Because the greater our harvest, the greater of a blessing we can be. Notice:

For God, who gives seed to the farmer to plant, and later on, good crops to harvest and eat, will give you more and more seed to plant *and will make it grow so that you can give away more and more fruit from your harvest.*
- II Corinthians 9:10, *THE LIVING BIBLE*

Because all of chapters 8 and 9 are teaching about finances I'm going to take the liberty to insert the words "money" and "increase" to help bring out this truth:

For God, who gives money to the Christian to give, and later on, financial increase to live on, will give you more and more money to give and will make your money grow so that you can give away more and more money from your financial increase.

- II Corinthians 9:10
(my paraphrase from THE LIVING BIBLE)

That this is what Paul is teaching there can be no doubt. We can see progression in this verse. The harvest keeps getting bigger and bigger as we give more and more. Initially, God gives us some money to give. The harvest then grows. From that first harvest we now have more to live on *and* more to give. So we increase our giving. The second bigger harvest then grows. From that second harvest we now have even more to live on *and even more to give.* So we again increase our giving some more. The third harvest then grows, and from that third harvest we now have even more than the first or second harvest. So what do we do? We increase our giving some more. And the cycle continues over and over again and again. The very next verse then says:

Yes, God will GIVE YOU MUCH so that YOU CAN GIVE AWAY MUCH...

- II Corinthians 9:11

God wants us to give more and more so that He can multiply back to us more and more, so that in turn, we can give away even more. Our harvest is determined by our giving -- small produces small and big produces big. God is all in favor of big harvests, but He has to talk His people into giving away big. It's time for the people of God to become cheerful givers, not greedy takers. Takers fall backwards, givers spring forward.

CHAPTER
19

TITHES AND OFFERINGS KEEP GOOD THINGS HAPPENING IN OUR LIVES

...and prove me now herewith, saith the Lord of hosts, if I will not open you the windows of heaven, and pour you out a blessing...

- Malachi 3:10

God was telling the people in Malachi's day *why* they were in financial bondage, and *why* they were living under a financial curse, and *why* the devourer was having free reign in their finances, and *why* they weren't blessed with blessings running over. The people were not doing something, knowingly *or unknowingly,* that was keeping good things from happening in their lives.

I've become convinced that in many areas of our lives, the reason bad things are always around some people is not because bad things are continually happening, *but rather because good things have stopped happening.* For example, if we leave our front yard alone and not do anything about it, we realize what's going to happen to it. *Bad things, of course.* Weeds will start growing, crabgrass will start growing, dandelions will start growing, and the good grass will get choked out and start dying away.

Because this world is under a curse, the moment something starts to live it starts to die. A good yard is the result of a lot of hard work. We have to pull the weeds, we have to put fertilizer on the lawn, and we have to see to it that the good grass has a chance to grow. <u>A pretty lawn happens because a lot of good things happen.</u>

If we stop the good things from happening, if we stop the fertilizing, if we stop the weeding, the front lawn will go bad in a matter of weeks. A bad lawn is not the result of bad things happening. **A bad lawn is the result of good things that are no longer happening.**

You see, the curse is the absence of blessing. If you've been living under a curse financially, it simply means you haven't been blessed financially in a long time. But bring in the blessings and the curse has to leave. Bring in healing and sickness has to leave. Bring in prosperity and poverty has to leave.

Poverty is just simply the lack of prosperity.
Sickness is just simply the lack of healing.
Darkness is just simply the lack of light.
The curse is just simply the lack of blessing.

We can't get rid of the curse without some kind of a blessing taking place first. In Deuteronomy 28, God says, "Do this, and you'll be blessed. If you don't do this, you'll be cursed." It's called the curse of the law.

I've always been amused with people who say that God curses people. They say such things as, "*If you don't do what's right God will curse you.*" But no, God is not in the business of cursing people, God is in the business of blessing people.

188

The curse is already here. What happens is, if you do what God says to do God will bless you. But if you refuse to do what God says to do, as much as God would like to bless you, God can't bless disobedience. So if God isn't blessing you, that means there's not any blessing to override the curse that's here, therefore all you can experience is the curse. *So it's not that God curses people, it's just that God stops blessing these people.* **And if God isn't blessing them, there's nothing for them to experience except the curse that's already on this planet.**

A perfect analogy is light and darkness. Darkness is the absence of light. When light shows up darkness has to leave. When light leaves, darkness comes back. Darkness never determines what light is going to do, light always determines what darkness is going to do. There is never a struggle between light and darkness. If you walk into a dark room and turn on a light, you'll never see darkness struggling with the light trying to stay. Darkness is only possible if there's no light.

The smallest matchstick is more powerful than any cave of darkness. If our sun would completely burn out and our whole universe would be engulfed in complete darkness, the smallest matchstick would still be more powerful than an entire universe of darkness. If you strike that match, regardless of how many millions of miles of darkness surround you, the darkness around you will leave when that match is struck.

Thus, the way to overcome darkness is turn on a light. *Likewise, the way to overcome the curse is to turn on a blessing.* Just as you can't get rid of darkness without a light, you can't get rid of the curse without a blessing. But the curse never determines what a blessing is going to do. The blessing always determines what the curse is go-

189

ing to do. Again, the curse is just simply the absence of God's blessing. But when God blesses, the curse is overridden.

The reason the people Malachi was writing to were living under a curse was because God hadn't been blessing them. Why? Because they hadn't been tithing and giving offerings. Their failure to tithe and give offerings resulted in God withholding His blessing. As a result, they were living under a financial curse.

The cure, though, was simple -- resume tithes and offerings. If they would begin or resume their tithes and offerings, God would see to it that the devourer would be rebuked and that blessings would come. With the return of the blessings the curse would then no longer be a problem. *Tithes and offerings keep good things happening in our lives.*

CHAPTER
20

HOW DO WE ROB GOD?

Will a man rob God? Yet ye have robbed me...
- Malachi 3:8

There are two ways to look at this verse. Of course, without a doubt, when we fail to tithe and give offerings we rob God. But *how* do we rob God? There are two ways -- **1)** We rob God by keeping in our possession what God says belongs to Him, and **2)** when we fail to tithe and give offerings **we rob God of the opportunity to rebuke the devourer off of our finances and bless us.**

Incidentally, take notice that BOTH tithes AND offerings are important to God. When the people asked, "Wherein have we robbed thee?", God's answer to them was, "In tithes *and* offerings" (Mal. 3:8). Many have thought they were robbing God if they failed to tithe, but actually, we're robbing God if we fail to tithe AND give offerings. Verses 8 and 9 do not tell us the people were under a curse because they didn't tithe, it says they were under a curse because they didn't tithe *and* give offerings. The fact is, financial success will never come without our doing *both.*

191

1. When we fail to tithe and give offerings we rob God by keeping in our possession what God says belongs to Him.

This is the most obvious understanding of Malachi 3:8. We rob God by not returning to God what God claims is His. Leviticus 27:30 tells us the tithe belongs to God. The option to do with the tithe what _we_ want to do is not ours. Malachi 3:10 is very specific:

Bring ye *all* the tithes into the *storehouse*, that there may be meat in *mine* house...

Notice that _all_ of the tithe goes to the storehouse, not 50% of the tithe to the storehouse and 50% of the tithe to _your_ house. God plainly said, "that there may be meat in *mine* house," not *your* house, or your children's house, but 100% of the tithe into the _storehouse_. When we put the tithe into the storehouse, it's a blessing to the church, and it's a means for God to bless the tither.

Understand this -- God does not want 10 percent of your income to make it more _difficult_ on you. God wants 10 percent of your income to make it *more easy* on you. Some people have the mistaken idea that God is trying to make things hard on us, like God is saying that 100% of our money is too easy to live on. So God is going to take 10% of it away and make us live on only 90%. Then to make it even more difficult on us, He requires us to give offerings as well.

Sad to say, some people have been taught verses 8 and 9 of Malachi 3 real good, I mean, fire and brimstone messages about robbing God, but they were not taught verses 10, 11, and 12 about how God wanted to bless their finances (see page 146).

Even worse, some people were taught it was a _sin_ if a Christian had too much money. To actually say that God _wanted_ to be involved in their finances, and that God wanted to _increase_ their finances, was to somehow make God's hands seem filthy, as if God was lowering His standards, doing something disgusting. So these people were taught it was okay for God to _take_ their money, but it wasn't okay for God to _bless_ their money. So again, they were taught verses 8 and 9, but they weren't taught verses 10, 11, and 12.

But the truth is, the whole purpose of verse 8 and 9 was to get ALL of God's people to verses 10, 11, and 12. And to not teach verses 10, 11, and 12 is just as wrong in the sight of God as not preaching John 3:16. It's not right to ignore either scripture. Both scriptures point to a miraculous involvement on God's part in our lives. And this leads into the second way verse 8 can be understood.

2. Failing to tithe and give offerings robs God of the opportunity to bless His people.

It's important to realize that God is a God of _blessing_, He is a God of _abundance_, and He is a God of _liberally_ supplying and _filling to the full_ our every need (Phil 4:19, Amplified Bible). Again, God doesn't want to _take_ things from us, He wants to _receive_ things from us, _so that in turn He can work a miracle and get involved in our finances_.

When we fail to tithe and give offerings we rob God of the opportunity to rebuke the devourer off of our finances (v.10). We rob God of the opportunity to open the windows of heaven in our lives. And we rob God of the

193

opportunity to pour us out a blessing where we don't have enough room to contain it all.

GOD'S HEART IS TO BLESS

You see, God **wants** to rebuke Satan off of our finances so much. God **wants** to open the windows of heaven in our lives so much. God **wants** to pour us out an incredibly huge blessing so much. *But if we fail to tithe and give offerings we're robbing God of these opportunities to bless us.*

It's important to realize that God wants to bless us *more than we want to be blessed.* God wants to heal us more than we want to be healed. God wants to fill us with His Spirit more than we want to be filled. *And God wants to bless our finances more than we want our finances blessed.*

Tithes and offerings don't make it *harder* on us, tithes and offerings make it *easier* on us. It opens the door for God to work in our finances. It's not something disgusting, it's something miraculous. God *wants* to be involved in our finances, but again, if we fail to tithe and give offerings we rob God of these opportunities to open doors of promotion for us.

I don't know about you, but I don't want to rob God of any opportunity to bless me. *The truth is, when I rob God, I'm robbing me.* Quite frankly, I'm not hurting anyone but me. And if there's one person we need to be friends to, it's ourselves. I don't want to hurt me, and neither do I want to rob me. ***But yet I rob me if I rob God.***

HOW DO WE ROB GOD?

It all comes down to the fact of what our conception of God is, who He is and what He's like. If we think God is a "mean" God, an ogre, we're more apt to shy away from God and not trust Malachi 3. If we have a bad image of God (and it's unfortunate the bad image ignorant preachers have put into the minds of their people for hundreds of years), we won't release our faith in God.

Quite frankly, it's amazing to me how God has been able to bless as many people as He has with as much of the disgusting preaching that's gone on in some circles. Many, many people have the idea that God makes people sick, that God kills their parents, or that He kills their children, or that He causes tornados and hurricanes and floods and disasters. _But God is not the author of these kinds of tragedies._ John 10:10 tells us that _the thief,_ not God, _the thief_ comes to steal, to kill, and to destroy. Jesus then said, "But I've come that they might have life, _and that they might have life more abundantly._" You see, anything that steals, kills, or destroys is _not from God_, it's from the devil. _God is in the business of blessing people._

Because so many preachers haven't preached this the people can't believe. The apostle Paul said, "_how shall they believe if they have not heard? and how shall they hear without a preacher_" (Romans 10:14)? In other words, if it's not preached it can't be heard, and if it can't be heard it can't be believed.

This is why Malachi chapter 3 has to be preached _in a positive manner._ It's important to realize that verses 10, 11, and 12 are what God is looking to do in our lives. And verses 8 and 9 are the means that God uses to bring about the blessings of verses 10, 11, and 12. God wants our households to be a delightsome land. God wants other people to realize that God has blessed us. God wants to rebuke the devourer in our lives. And God wants to bless us so much where we don't have room enough to contain it all. To the one who tithes and gives offerings there's no such thing as a dead end job, a promotionless job, or a fixed income.

CHAPTER
21

LIVING IN ABUNDANCE

...good measure, pressed down, and shaken together, and running over...

- Luke 6:38

...and pour you out a blessing, that there shall not be room enough to receive it.

- Malachi 3:10

...shall reap also bountifully.

- II Corinthians 9:6

The bottom line for prosperity is for the establishing of the gospel in every nation, every tongue, and every tribe. God wants every person to have the repeated opportunity to hear the gospel of the Lord Jesus Christ. Matthew 24: 14 says that when every nation gets the gospel preached to them the end will then come.

And this gospel of the kingdom shall be preached in ALL the world for a witness unto ALL nations; and then shall the end come.

- Matthew 24:14

PIECING TOGETHER THE PROSPERITY PUZZLE

It takes a lot of money to print Christian witnessing tracts, support missionaries, buy TV and radio time, buy airplane tickets to preach, rent auditoriums, print Christian teaching books, etc. Quite frankly, it's amazing to me how much has been accomplished with the shoestring budgets many ministries have had to operate under.

Christianity is now the fastest growing religion in the world. In China I've heard estimates of between 15,000 Chinese upwards to 50,000 Chinese getting saved *every single day.* If we would purchase enough tracts so that each Chinese person could have just _one_ tract in their own language or dialect, our first purchase would be for a _billion_ copies! Think about that. And that's only for _one_ tract _per person_. And I think they need at least 10 tracts per person on a _yearly_ basis. Plus, they need Bibles in the Chinese language. That's one billion Bibles right there.!

Then what about India? What about Thailand? What about Mongolia? What about the Ukraine? What about Russia? What about Venezuela? What about Brazil? There are so many Bibles in different languages that need to be printed. There are so many Christian teaching publications that need to be printed. There are so many Christian television and radio stations that need to be built. We haven't even begun to scratch the surface of what *needs* to be done.

What about crusades? Do you realize how much it costs to rent auditoriums and coliseums? Then purchasing advertising -- mail outs, radio, TV, etc. And to think that that is only one city in a country of thousands of cities. How many more millions need to be reached in that one country alone?

Once we get them saved they need to be taught. Church buildings need to go up. Pastors need to be trained. Each country needs preachers who speak in their own native language. Thus, Bible schools need to go up. What kind of money are we looking at here?

As you can see, something has to change. It's always been sad to me to see how many of our missionaries have been treated by many of our churches. Think about how they have had to live their lives. They live away from home, away from their kin, away from everything they hold dear. And what do they do? They spend their whole lives living in a foreign country, with different customs, with a different language, without many of the modern day conveniences you and I take for granted. When they do get a 3 month reprieve, what do they end up having to do? They have to travel at home going from state to state, church to church, trying to drum up more financial support so that they can go back to live in a foreign country. They never get the chance to just lay on a beach somewhere and rest.

I think this has to change. We need to be so blessed financially that we can support our missionaries, *and support them well.* When they get a 3-month reprieve, they should be able to have some R&R. Let them enjoy the beach, let them have some time with their kin, let them have some free time for spiritual refreshing. They should be able to attend any preaching conference they want to, anywhere in the country at our expense. *If we can get them charged up, think what a greater blessing they could be to the country they're ministering in.* Instead of being drained, exhausted, and running on nervous energy, they could go back refreshed, rested, and spiritually charged up.

We're living in a day when extreme amounts of money are needed. This thinking of God only meeting the needs of our four and no more has to be expelled from our minds. This is a day when we need to believe God to meet the needs of our four, *and then a whole lot more!* If we are blessed we can then be a blessing.

God is waiting for us to make the necessary changes so that He can bring to pass in our lives this power to get wealth for the establishing of His covenant. God certainly doesn't have a problem with us living nice and driving nice. That's a part of what this book has been about. God *wants* us to live nice and drive nice, but He definitely wants our priorities to see the fields that are ripe for the harvest. We need to start thinking big and believing big. Much needs to be accomplished in the world, *and we are the vessels that God is going to use to bring it through.*

It's absolutely necessary that the Church World be able to have billions and billions, even trillions and trillions of dollars at their disposal. Since Jesus instructed us to go into all of the world with the gospel, and since it takes billions of dollars (trillions of dollars, actually, to do it right), we, the Church, need to have this kind of money at our fingertips. God wants *us* to prosper, and to prosper *exceedingly*.

We need more modern day Davids, more Jobs, more Abrahams, more Hezekiahs. We need more believers like Joseph of Arimathea. When a church project, a missionary project, or an evangelistic project comes up, we need people who will stand up and say, "*Let me take care of this one. Here's a check for 10 million dollars.*" Several years ago a nationally known minister was short on a certain project by about 8 million dollars. What happened? *One* man wrote a check for 8 million dollars and gave it to him!

200

It's high time for the people *in the Church* all over the world to be able to write these kinds of checks. God has a plan to prosper His people. He's got all kinds of different ideas to give His people to bring in vast amounts of money. *But these ideas will only come to people who are tithers and givers.* I want to see God's people arise from the depths of defeat and debt and move into the promised land of God's overflowing abundance. If you know Jesus Christ as your Lord and Savior ***you are such a person.*** God wants **you** to experience exceeding abundantly above all that you can ask or think financially. **You** are one of the many vessels in these last days God wants to use to help be a part of this great end-time revival.

NOTES